The Complete
COOKBOOK
for
TEEN CHEFS

200 Super Easy, Fast, and Delicious Recipes
to Level Up Your Kitchen Game
For Teens, Students, Young Chefs and Beginners

OLIVIA S. LAWRENCE

© Copyright 2023 - All rights reserved.

The content contained within this book may not be reproduced, duplicated or transmitted without direct written permission from the author or the publisher.

Under no circumstances will any blame or legal responsibility be held against the publisher, or author, for any damages, reparation, or monetary loss due to the information contained within this book, either directly or indirectly.

Legal Notice:

This book is copyright protected. It is only for personal use. You cannot amend, distribute, sell, use, quote or paraphrase any part, or the content within this book, without the consent of the author or publisher.

Disclaimer Notice:

Please note the information contained within this document is for educational and entertainment purposes only. All effort has been executed to present accurate, up to date, reliable, complete information. No warranties of any kind are declared or implied. Readers acknowledge that the author is not engaged in the rendering of legal, financial, medical or professional advice. The content within this book has been derived from various sources. Please consult a licensed professional before attempting any techniques outlined in this book.

By reading this document, the reader agrees that under no circumstances is the author responsible for any losses, direct or indirect, that are incurred as a result of the use of the information contained within this document, including, but not limited to, errors, omissions, or inaccuracies.

TABLE OF CONTENTS

APPETIZERS 2

Fried Carrots 3
Crispy Mozzarella 4
Melted Cheese Sandwich 5
Caprese Bruschetta 6
Salmon Bruschetta 7
Stuffed Mozzarella 8
Bruschetta with Figs and Ham 9
Hard-Boiled Eggs 10
Soft-Boiled Eggs 11
Eggs with Avocado and Smoked Salmon 12
Smoked Salmon Mousse 13
Baked Scallops 14
Tuna fillet in a Walnut-Pistachio Crust 15
Colorful Salmon with Vegetables 16
Mozzarella and Crab Cubes 17
Swordfish with Mustard 18
Smoked Swordfish with Arugula and Apple Salad 19
Spicy Shrimp 20
Toast with Butter and Sardines 21
Fried Tofu 22

FIRST COURSES 23

Spaghetti with Garlic, Oil and Chili 25
Noodles with 4 Cheeses 26
Spaghetti with Tuna 27
Spicy Spaghetti 28
Pasta with Anchovies and Cherry Tomatoes 29
Noodles with Pecorino Cheese and Pea Cream 30
Noodles with Tuna and Ricotta 31
Rice Plate 32
Noodles with Pesto and Bacon 33
Noodles with Shallot and Salmon 34
Noodles with Zucchini, Thyme, and Lemon 35
Spaghetti Carbonara 36
Spaghetti with Cheese and Pepper 37
Noodles with Guanciale and Pecorino Cheese 38
Penne with Cream and Ham 39
Noodles with Zucchini 40
Spinach Spätzle with Bacon and Cream 41
Creamy Pasta with Pepper Flavor 42
Noodles with Onions and Salmon 43

Risotto with Parmesan Cheese 44
Noodles with Ricotta 45
Noodles with Gorgonzola and Olives 46
Noodles with Tuna 47
Noodles with Gorgonzola and Walnuts 48
Noodles with Zucchini and Eggs 49
Noodles with Red Pesto 50
Salmon Risotto 51
Crispy Spaghetti with Sardines 52
Noodles with Lemon and Tuna 53
Noodles with Radicchio and Bacon 54
Spaghetti with Spinach and Ricotta 55
Fettuccine with Truffles 56
Noodles with Gorgonzola 57
Champagne-Risotto 58
Farmer's Pasta 59
Curry-Rice 60
Noodles with Cherry Tomatoes and Cream Cheese 61
Penne with Sausage 62
Mountain-Risotto 63
Neapolitan Pasta 64
Pasta with Peas and Tuna 65
Pasta with Creamy Broccoli 66
Pasta with Breadcrumbs 67
Pasta with Cream and Onions 68
Lime Pasta 69
Gnocchi with Pea Cream 70
Cold Pasta with Cherry Tomatoes and Ricotta Cheese 71
Spaghetti with Sardines, sun-dried Tomatoes, and Crispy Breadcrumbs 72
Linguine with Pesto 73
Spaghetti Carbonara (Version with Fish) 74
Pumpkin-Gnocchi 75
Penne with Ham, Cream and Peas 76
Noodles with Fresh Salmon and Red Onions 77
Smoked Pasta 78
Spaghetti with Clams and Beans 79
Pasta with Tuna and Arungula Pesto 80
Pasta with Egg and Cheese 81
Penne Pasta with Arugula and Chickpea Cream 82
Pasta with Cherry Tomatoes and Anchovies 83
Spaghetti with Anchovies, Flavored with Orange 84

MAIN COURSES 85

Crispy Salmon 87
Chicken Breasts in Milk 88
Mushroom Escalopes 89
Chicken with Soy Sauce 90
Lemon Escalopes 91

Sole with Milk	92
Meat in Sauce	93
Chicken Strips	94
Baked Cod Fillets	95
Swordfish with Olives	96
Eggplant Cordon Bleu	97
Sautéed Beef with Arugula and Cherry Tomatoes	98
Beef Strips	99
Salmon Fillets with Black Olives and Cherry Tomatoes	100
Swordfish Rolls	101
Stuffed Chicken Rolls	102
Pork with Marsala Wine	103
Chicken Breast with Cornflakes	104
Pork Tenderloin	105
Pan-seared Cod Filet	106
Bolognese Cutlet	107
Kale-Burger	108
Fried Calamari	109
Chicken nuggets with Yogurt	110
Pork tenderloin with Honey and Ginger	111
Eggs and Peas	112
Salmon steak with Tomatoes and Thyme	113
Cutlet with Ham and Cheese	114
Chicken Breasts with Mustard and Herbs	115
Turkey Cutlets	116
Beef Carpaccio with Arugola and Parmesan	117
Scrambled Eggs	118
Salmon Burgers	119
Peppers with Eggs	120
Scampi with Tomatoes and Breadcrumbs	121
Turkey Rolls	122
Plaice Fillets in Sauce	123
Pork Chops with Lemon	124
Plaice Fillets with Herbs	125
Cod Burger	126
Veal with Vegetables	127
Seafood Skewers	128
Chicken Cutlets with Balsamic Vinegar	129
Shrimp with Coconut Aroma	130
Flavored Sliced Beef	131
Sliced Beef with Balsamic Vinegar	132
Chicken Skewers	133
Beef Slices with Tomato	134
Fried Chicken Wings	135
Currywurst	136
Spicy Sausages	137
Pan-Seared Sole with Butter and Sage	138
Burger-Trio	139

Veal with Saffron 140
Aromatized Beef.. 141
Plaice meatballs 142
Wrapped Sausages... 143
Swordfish Tartar 144
Bites of Pollock 145
Pock with Roquefort 146

SIDE DISHES 147

Pan-Fried Fennel... 149
Grilled Oyster Mushrooms.. 150
French Fries 151
Rosemary Roasted Pumpkin.. 152
Cauliflower puree 153
Roasted Broccoli 154
Roasted Soybean Sprouts 155
Fried Mushrooms 156
Fried Artichokes with Mustard 157
Seasoned Carrots 158
Roasted Brussels Sprouts 159
Microwave potatoes 160
Potatoes and Peppers 161
Fried Zucchini... 162
Fried Cauliflower 163

SALADS.. 166

Artichoke Salad 167
Chickpea Salad 168
Salad with Chicken and Zucchini 169
Salad with Pears, Arugula, Parmesan and Walnuts... 170
Salad with Pears and Gorgonzola Cheese 171
Cucumber Salad.. 172
Salad with Sardines, Cherry Tomatoes and Eggs.. 173
Apple-Chicken Salad.. 174
Salad with Tuna, Carrots, Corn and Green Beans 175
Crispy Salad.. 176

ONE-PLATE MEALS 178

Classic Sandwich 179
Tacos.. 180
Croque Madame.. 181
Spicy Sandwich with Tuna, Olive Pesto and Goat Cheese.. 182
Piadine with Corn and Chicken 183
Couscous with Feta, Watermelon, and Tomatoes 184
Piadina with Gorgonzola, Prosciutto and Tomatoes 185
Piadina with Stracchino Cheese and Zucchini 186

Double Cheeseburger..187
Mozzarella and Tomato Omelette...188
Bowl with Quinoa, Cheese, Apple and Red Fruits..189
Bowl with Salmon, Crispy Bread, and Avocado..190
Tuna and Zucchini Carpaccio..191
Quinoa Eggplant and Mint 192
Tacos with Shrimp and Kale..193

DESSERTS 196

Hot Chocolate 197
Candied Almonds 198
French Toast..199
Pancakes 200
Cake in a Cup 201
Yogurt Pancakes 202
Berry Yogurt Cup 203
Tiramisu Truffles 204
Waffles...205
Oatmeal with Hazelnuts and Apples 206
Chia Pudding 207
Cappuccino Milkshake...208
Chocolate Cup with Mascarpone and Meringues 209
Sweet Rice and Lemon Pancakes...210
Chocolate and Avocado Mousse 211
Strawberry Milkshake 212
Caramelized Bananas 213
Lactose-free Cocoa and Cinnamon Pudding..214
Pistachio Ice Cream without an Ice Cream Maker..215
Raspberry Panna Cotta 216

APPETIZERS

Fried Carrots

Level: Easy
Preparation: 3 min
Cooking time: 10 min
Servings: 2

INGREDIENTS

- 1.75 oz Parmesan cheese
- 9 oz Carrots
- 1 tablespoon Paprika
- Fine salt
- Thyme
- Rosemary
- Redberry jam
- Peanut oil

METHOD

1. Start with the breading.
2. Finely chop the rosemary and mix it together with the grated cheese.
3. Chop the thyme, mix everything together with the paprika.
4. Now move on to the carrots.
5. Peel and trim them, then divide them in half or into 4 parts (depending on the size).
6. Cut the parts into sticks about 0.5 inch.
7. Finally cut into sticks about 0.5 inch.
8. Dip the carrots in the breading and make sure it sticks well.
9. Fry the breaded carrots in a pot with boiling oil at 360°.
10. After about 1 minute the sticks will be golden brown, then you can drain them on paper towel.
11. Season again with what is left of the breading and salt and continue frying all the other sticks.
12. Serve with redberry jam.

Crispy Mozzarella

Difficulty: very easy
Preparation: 12 min
Cooking time: 9 min
Servings: 12 pieces

INGREDIENTS

- 9 oz Mozzarella
- 2 teaspoon Whole milk
- 1 medium egg
- Breadcrumbs
- Wheat flour
- Peanut oil
- Salt
- Black pepper

METHOD

1. Cut the mozzarella into about 0.75 inch slices and then cut them into cubes. Let the cubes drip off and dry them in a sieve.
2. Sprinkle the mozzarella cubes in a bowl with flour, so that each cube is completely covered.
3. In another bowl, beat the egg with salt, pepper, and a little milk.
4. Dip the mozzarella pieces in the mixture and let them soak well.
5. Then dip the pieces in breadcrumbs.
6. Repeat the process a second time, so that the pieces become crispier.
7. Make sure the mozzarella pieces are perfectly covered with the breading.
8. Your mozzarella is now ready to fry.
9. Pour the frying oil into a large pan.
10. Before putting the mozzarella in the oil, make sure it has the right temperature; just put a little breadcrumbs in the oil. If it sizzles, you can continue frying 3 or 4 mozzarella pieces at a time.
11. Let them fry for a few minutes (or until they are golden brown).
12. Be careful not to puncture them.
13. Let it dry on absorbent paper.
14. Remove excess oil with more paper towels.

Melted Cheese Sandwich

Difficulty: very easy
Preparation: 6 min
Cooking time: 7 min
Servings: 2

INGREDIENTS

- 3 oz Cheddar cheese
- 4 oz White bread (4 slices)
- Room temperature butter

METHOD

1. First, cut the bread into slices, you need 4 slices of about 0.5 inch thick.
2. Butter all 4 slices on one side only.
3. Grate the cheddar and generously spread it on 2 slices, on the unbuttered side.
4. Cover them with the other slices of bread, with the buttered side facing out, so that the two sandwiches have cheese inside and butter outside.
5. Heat a non-stick pan and place the sandwich on medium heat.
6. Cover it for a few minutes with a lid.
7. Turn the sandwich over and crush it to speed up the melting of the cheese, and cover it for another minute.
8. Wait until the cheese is fully melted, then the sandwich is ready.
9. Cut it in half to form two triangles.

Caprese Bruschetta

Difficulty: very easy
Preparation: 9 min
Cooking time: 6 min
Servings: 2 people

INGREDIENTS

- 4.5 oz Mozzarella
- 2 slices of bread
- 5 tomatoes
- 4 basil leaves
- 1 pinch of oregano
- 6 black olives
- 1 clove of garlic
- Extra virgin olive oil
- Salt

METHOD

1. Cut 2 slices of bread 0.75 inch thick and toast them on both sides in a pan. Bring them to a golden color.
2. Rub one clove of garlic over both slices.
3. Set the bread aside and gather the ingredients for the dressing.
4. Drain the Mozzarella and cut it into small cubes. Cut the cherry tomatoes into 4 pieces.
5. Add mozzarella, black olives, and cherry tomatoes to a bowl, add chopped basil, oregano, salt, and cold-pressed olive oil.
6. Stir to mix all the flavors.
7. Spread the mixture on the bread slices and season with a little more olive oil before serving.

Salmon Bruschetta

Difficulty: very easy
Preparation: 16 min
Servings: 2 people

INGREDIENTS

- 7 oz Multi-grain bread
- 6.5 oz Smoked salmon
- 2 tablespoons Butter
- 2 tablespoons Capers
- 2 tablespoons Arugula
- 1 Lemon
- Coarse salt

METHOD

1. Cut the bread into slices that should be about 0.5 inch thick; place them on the cutting board, halve them and spread them with a layer of butter (about 0.18 oz).
2. Do the same for all bread slices.
3. Cut the salmon into slices, each slice should be about 2 tablespoons and as big as a bread slice.
4. Arrange the salmon slices on the bread and add arugula (about 0.14 oz per slice) to each piece.
5. Add a teaspoon of capers (about 0.14 oz) to each slice and finally add coarse salt and lemon juice.

Stuffed Mozzarella

Difficulty: very easy
Preparation: 9 min
Servings: 2 people

INGREDIENTS

- 2 Mozzarella (4.4 oz each)
- 1.5 oz Cherry tomatoes
- Extra virgin olive oil
- Black pepper
- Salt
- Oregano
- Basil, a few leaves

METHOD

1. Hollow out the inside of the two mozzarellas, cube the contents and set them aside.
2. Dry the mozzarellas by leaving them with the opening facing down.
3. Cut the tomatoes into four pieces and put them in a bowl, add almost all of the mozzarella cubes, and keep the rest for the presentation of the dish.
4. Season with olive oil, salt, pepper, dried oregano, and basil leaves.
5. Mix everything together.
6. Fill the mozzarellas with the filling mixture and place a few remaining mozzarella cubes on the plate!

Bruschetta with Figs and Ham

Difficulty: easy
Preparation: 9 min
Cooking time: 6 min
Servings: 2 pieces

INGREDIENTS

- 3.5 oz Figs
- 3.5 oz Bread
- 3.5 oz Cream cheese
- 1.7 oz Ham (4 slices)
- 2 teaspoon Honey
- 2 strands of chives
- Black pepper
- Salt

METHOD

1. Cut two slices of bread of the same thickness.
2. Heat a grill and toast the two slices on both sides for a few minutes.
3. Set the bruschetta aside.
4. Take the cream cheese.
5. Cut the chives after washing them thoroughly.
6. Combine them in a bowl with the cream cheese and mix the ingredients well.
7. Season with salt and pepper.
8. Prepare the figs: wash them, halve them and then cut them into three pieces. Spread honey on the entire surface.
9. Grill on the hot grill for a few seconds on both sides, turning the slices with kitchen tongs.
10. Now you can assemble the bruschetta.
11. Take the cream cheese and spread it on the bread slices.
12. Place 2 slices of ham and fig slices on each slice.
13. Repeat the process for the second slice, of course.

Hard-Boiled Eggs

Difficulty: easy
Preparation: 3 min
Cooking time: 8 min
Servings: 2 pieces

INGREDIENTS

- 2 Eggs at room temperature

METHOD

1. Quickly add the eggs to a pot of water, there should be enough water to fully submerge the eggs.
2. Bring the water to a boil and continue to boil for 8 minutes.
3. Now, drain the eggs and cool them under cold running water.
4. Tap the top of the egg lightly to crack the shell and then begin to remove the shell.

Soft-Boiled Eggs

Difficulty: easy
Preparation: 3 min
Cooking time: 4 min
Servings: 2 pieces

INGREDIENTS

- 2 Eggs

METHOD

1. Bring a pot of water to a boil.
2. Gently lower the eggs into the boiling water and let them cook for 4 minutes. If the eggs are straight from the refrigerator, cook them for 4 minutes, if they are at room temperature, cook them for 3 minutes.
3. Once the cooking time is up, gently shake the eggs and transfer them to an egg cup, tapping the top of the egg with a spoon to crack the shell.
4. Carefully remove the shell and peel off the egg white until the yolk (which should be semi-liquid) is visible.

Eggs with Avocado and Smoked Salmon

Difficulty: Easy
Preparation: 4 min
Cooking time: 11 min
Servings: 2 people

INGREDIENTS

- 1.75 oz Smoked salmon
- 2 Eggs
- 1 Avocado
- 1 Lime
- 3 Stalks of chives
- Extra virgin olive oil
- Black pepper
- Crushed pink pepper
- Salt

METHOD

1. Grate the lime zest and keep it in a bowl. Cut the chives and set them aside.
2. Halve the avocado (you will need 14 oz avocado for 2 people), remove the pit, squeeze some lime over it and scoop out the flesh with a spoon (tip: cut the flesh horizontally and vertically first, it will be easier to remove).
3. Place a slice of salmon on each avocado half, season with salt and pepper and add the lime zest.
4. Heat a pan with olive oil and crack in the eggs without stirring. Cook for a few minutes (max. 3).
5. Once the eggs are cooked, place them on top of the avocado. Season with crushed pink pepper and chopped chives.

Smoked Salmon Mousse

Difficulty: easy
Preparation: 16 min
Servings: 3 people

INGREDIENTS

- 1/2 cup Ricotta cheese
- 2 oz Smoked salmon
- 1/4 cup Heavy cream
- 3 sprigs Dill
- Salt and pepper to taste
- 7 slices of black bread
- Caviar
- Dill

METHOD

1. Chop the Ricotta cheese and smoked salmon in a food processor until well combined.
2. Wash and chop the dill, then add it to the food processor, pulse until well combined. Season with salt and pepper to taste.
3. In a separate bowl, whip the heavy cream until stiff peaks form. Gently fold the whipped cream into the salmon mixture.
4. Toast the slices of black bread in a pan until crispy.
5. Spread the salmon mixture onto the toasted bread slices and top with caviar and additional dill. Serve and enjoy!

Baked Scallops

Difficulty: Very easy
Preparation: 14 min
Cooking time: 14 min
Servings: 2 people

INGREDIENTS

- 1/2 cup breadcrumbs
- 1 tablespoon extra virgin olive oil
- 4 scallops
- 1 lemon zest
- Parsley
- Thyme
- 1/4 teaspoon black pepper
- 1/4 teaspoon salt

METHOD

1. In a blender, combine breadcrumbs, oil, salt, pepper, herbs, parsley, thyme, and some grated lemon zest.
2. Toss the scallops in the breadcrumb mixture.
3. Place the scallops on a baking sheet and bake in a preheated oven at 375°F for about 15 minutes or until a crispy crust forms.

Tuna fillet in a Walnut-Pistachio Crust

Difficulty level: Easy
Preparation time: 11 min
Cooking time: 6 min
Servings: 2 people

INGREDIENTS

- 7 oz Tuna fillet
- 1.5 oz Soy sauce
- 2 tablespoons raw and unsalted pistachios
- 2 tablespoons walnuts

METHOD

1. Use a food processor to pulse the nuts and pistachios (peeled) until you achieve a fairly coarse texture. Transfer to a bowl. Pour the soy sauce into a separate bowl and coat both sides of the tuna fillet. Dip the fillet into the breading and make sure it is fully coated.
2. Heat a pan and cook the tuna for a few minutes on each side, using tongs to flip the fillet. Be careful not to cook it too long, the fillet should remain pink.
3. Once the fillet is cooked, slice it into about 0.75 inch thick slices. Serve with an additional drizzle of soy sauce.

Colorful Salmon with Vegetables

Difficulty level: very easy
Preparation time: 16 min
Servings: 2 people

INGREDIENTS

- 9 oz salmon fillet
- 1.35 oz white wine vinegar
- 5 oz water
- 1/2 stalk celery
- 1/2 red onion
- 1/2 carrot
- Pink pepper
- Black pepper
- Salt

METHOD

1. The ideal salmon for this recipe is Norwegian, otherwise you'll have to freeze and chill it for safety reasons.
2. Peel the onion and cut it in half, then slice the two halves into slices.
3. Wash the celery stalk well and remove the leaves (both the side and the outer ones). Use a vegetable peeler to remove the outer layer of strings. Now you can also slice the celery into thin strips.
4. Take a bowl and add water, white wine vinegar, salt, pink pepper, black pepper, and the previously cut vegetables (celery, carrot, onion).
5. Remove the salmon fillet from the bones using kitchen tongs and then slice it into thin slices.
6. Add the salmon pieces to the previously made mixture and cover the bowl with plastic wrap. Let it marinate in the fridge for a few hours.
7. After two hours, the salmon has absorbed all the flavors and the dish is ready!

Mozzarella and Crab Cubes

Difficulty level: Easy
Preparation time: 14 min
Servings: 2

INGREDIENTS

- 7 oz red shrimp
- 0.8 oz Mozzarella (in chunks)
- Zest of half a lemon
- 1.2 teaspoon extra virgin olive oil
- Basil
- Black pepper
- Salt

METHOD

1. Clean the red shrimp and then remove the head, legs, and tail.
2. Remove the black part from the shrimp's back (the intestine).
3. Once the shrimp are clean, chop them with a knife (without overdoing it).
4. Season the shrimp in a bowl, add olive oil, salt, and pepper. Add the chopped basil and mix well.
5. Drain the Mozzarella chunks by halving them and patting them dry with a kitchen towel.
6. Grate the lemon zest into a bowl.
7. Now you have all the ingredients ready: Take an appetizer spoon and add a piece of Mozzarella and the shrimp.

Swordfish with Mustard

Difficulty: very easy
Preparation: 9 min
Servings: 2

INGREDIENTS

- 7 oz smoked swordfish carpaccio
- 2 tablespoons coarse mustard
- 2 teaspoon pine nuts
- 1 bunch parsley
- 1 teaspoon white wine vinegar
- Extra virgin olive oil
- Salt

METHOD

1. Start by preparing the sauce: in a blender, puree the parsley with pine nuts, a teaspoon of white wine vinegar and the extra virgin olive oil. You should get a creamy and homogeneous mixture.
2. Put the sauce in a small bowl and add two tablespoons of mustard and salt.
3. Arrange the swordfish carpaccio on a salad layer, drizzle with oil and pour over the prepared sauce. Let it rest for at least 20 minutes.
4. Serve the dish at room temperature.

Smoked Swordfish with Arugula and Apple Salad

Difficulty level: easy
Preparation: 9 min
Servings: 2

INGREDIENTS

- 9 oz apples
- 2 oz arugula
- 3.5 oz smoked swordfish carpaccio
- 2 oz Greek yogurt
- 1.5 tbsp chives
- 1 tablespoon coarse mustard
- 2 tablespoons extra virgin olive oil
- Juice of half a lemon
- 1/2 clove of garlic
- Black pepper
- Salt

METHOD

1. Start with the sauce: Press the garlic into a small bowl and add lemon juice and mustard.
2. Add the yogurt and olive oil and mix everything into a smooth mixture. Season with salt and pepper.
3. Cut the chives and set aside.
4. Peel the apples and cut off the top and bottom.
5. Cut the apples in half and then in half again (so each apple into 4 segments).
6. Remove the cores from each segment.
7. Cut the segments into very thin slices.
8. Take a bowl and add the arugula and apple slices. Season with oil, salt and pepper and place on a serving platter.
9. Lay the swordfish carpaccio on a salad bed and be creative when serving.
10. Pour over the prepared sauce and sprinkle with chives.

Spicy Shrimp

Difficulty: Easy
Preparation: 11 min
Cooking time: 5 min
Servings: 2

INGREDIENTS

- 8 oz. shrimp
- 1 clove of garlic
- ½ fresh chili pepper
- 3 tablespoons extra virgin olive oil
- Black pepper
- Salt

METHOD

1. Clean the shrimp, peel them, and remove the black thread from the intestine.
2. In a pan, fry two cloves of garlic in 3 tablespoons of olive oil over medium heat.
3. Wash the chili pepper, remove the stem and cut it in half to remove the seeds inside. Then, finely chop it and add it to the pan with the oil.
4. Add the shrimp and fry them on both sides for about 4 minutes.
5. Do not overcook them or they will become tough.
6. Season with salt and pepper to taste.

Toast with Butter and Sardines

Difficulty: Easy
Preparation: 4 min
Cooking: 9 min
Servings: 2

INGREDIENTS

- 1.75 oz drained spicy sardines in oil
- 2 slices homemade bread
- 1.5 oz salted butter
- 1 half peach
- Parsley

METHOD

1. Finely chop the parsley and melt the butter in a bowl until you have a creamy consistency, then add the parsley.
2. Wash the peach and cut it in half, remove the pit and then cut into slices and then into cubes.
3. Cut bread slices and toast them until they are crispy.
4. Spread the butter cream on the bread slices and add a spoonful of diced peaches and sardine fillets on top.

Fried Tofu

Difficulty level: very easy
Preparation: 11 min
Cooking time: 6 min
Servings: 4 people

INGREDIENTS

- 5.5 oz Tofu
- Sage
- Rosemary
- 2 tablespoons Soy sauce
- 5.5 oz Water
- 3.5 oz Wheat flour
- Salt
- 2 oz Breadcrumbs
- 1 teaspoon Rosemary (chopped)
- Salt

Oil

METHOD

1. Cut the tofu into 1 inch cubes.
2. Take a bowl and add soy sauce, rosemary, sage and the tofu cubes. Seal the bowl with plastic wrap to marinate.
3. Take the breadcrumbs and season them in a bowl with salt and chopped rosemary.
4. Prepare the batter: Mix flour (3.5 oz), salt and water (5.3 oz) in a bowl.
5. Fry the tofu: Heat the oil to 340°, take the tofu cubes out of the marinade and dip them in the batter, then coat them in breadcrumbs.
6. Fry a few pieces at a time for about 1 minute or until golden brown.
7. Let the cubes rest on absorbent kitchen paper.

FIRST COURSES

Spaghetti with Garlic, Oil and Chili

Difficulty level: very easy
Preparation: 6 min
Cooking time: 9 min
Servings: 2 people

INGREDIENTS

- 6 oz spaghetti
- 2 cloves of garlic
- 2.5 tablespoon extra virgin olive oil
- 1 chili
- Salt

METHOD

1. Boil a pot of water. Once it is boiling, add salt to the water and add the pasta.
2. Clean the garlic and cut the cloves in half. Slice the garlic very thinly. Do the same with the chili, discarding the stem.
3. Pour the oil into a large frying pan. Heat the oil on low heat and add the garlic and chili.
4. Cook for a few minutes on a very low flame, so that the spices do not burn.
5. Once the pasta is cooked (follow the instructions on the package), drain it and add it to the pan with the sauce.
6. Mix the pasta well by tossing it.

Noodles with 4 Cheeses

Difficulty level: easy
Preparation: 11 min
Cooking time: 14 min
Servings: 2 people

INGREDIENTS

- 6 oz Penne noodles
- 1.5 oz soft Taleggio cheese
- 1.5 oz Parmigiano-Reggiano cheese
- 2 oz Gorgonzola cheese
- 1.5 oz Gruyère cheese, grated
- 3.25 oz whole milk
- White pepper
- Salt

METHOD

1. Boil a pot of water. Once it boils, salt the water and add the noodles.
2. Meanwhile, grate the Gruyère cheese, cut the Taleggio cheese into small to medium size cubes, and cut the Gorgonzola cheese into small pieces.
3. Heat the milk in a pot on low heat. Once it is hot, add the Taleggio and Gorgonzola.
4. Melt everything together and stir slowly, then add the Gruyère cheese and grated Parmesan.
5. Mix everything together for an additional 30 seconds and then turn off the heat.
6. When the noodles are cooked, drain them and add them to the 4-cheese cream.
7. Season with pepper and/or salt, stir so that all ingredients combine, and then serve.

Spaghetti with Tuna

Difficulty level: very easy
Preparation: 6 min
Cooking time: 9 min
Servings: 2 people

INGREDIENTS

- 6 oz Spaghetti
- 7 oz peeled tomatoes
- Extra virgin olive oil
- 2.75 oz Tuna in cans
- 1/2 onion
- Basil
- Ground black pepper
- Salt

METHOD

1. Boil a pot of water, salted to taste. Drain the oil from the tuna can.
2. Slice the onion into very thin slices. Heat the oil in a small pan and add the onion slices.
3. Cook for a few minutes and stir often to prevent burning.
4. Crumble the tuna and add it to the pan, cook for 2/3 minutes.
5. Crush the peeled tomatoes with a fork and add them along with the tuna to the pan.
6. Cook the sauce for about 9 minutes.
7. Meanwhile, add the spaghetti to the boiling water and cook according to package instructions.
8. Once the spaghetti is cooked, drain it and add it to the pan with the sauce. Add pepper and basil.
9. Mix everything well.

Spicy Spaghetti

Difficulty level: very easy
Preparation: 9 min
Servings: 2 people

INGREDIENTS

- 6 oz Spaghetti
- 1 Dried Chili
- 1 clove of Garlic
- 1 tablespoon Extra Virgin Olive Oil
- 5.25 oz Tomato Sauce
- Basil

METHOD

1. Cook the sauce in a pot for about 9 minutes.
2. Cook the spaghetti in a pot of boiling, salted water according to the package instructions.
3. In the meantime, sauté a clove of garlic in oil for two minutes in another pan.
4. When the noodles are cooked, drain them and add them to the sauce. Chop the dried chili and add it to the noodles.
5. Mix for one minute and remove the garlic.
6. Season with salt and if you want, you can increase the heat so that the noodles lightly brown and become crispy.

Pasta with Anchovies and Cherry Tomatoes

Difficulty level: very easy
Preparation: 5 min
Cooking time: 11 min
Servings: 2 people

INGREDIENTS

- 7 oz Noodles (any type)
- 2.25 oz Cherry Tomatoes
- 2 Basil leaves
- 1.5 tablespoons Extra virgin olive oil
- 1 tablespoon Salt-cured Anchovies
- Chili
- 1 Garlic clove
- Salt

METHOD

1. Boil water in a pot.
2. When it boils, season with salt to taste.
3. In the meantime, you can continue with the sauce.
4. Wash the cherry tomatoes and cut them first in half and then in quarters, so that 4 slices are created per tomato.
5. Add a little oil and a garlic clove in a pan, let it turn golden yellow and then remove it from the pan.
6. Now clean the anchovies and put them in the pan to fry them in the oil.
7. When they are fried, add the cherry tomatoes.
8. Fry on high heat for a few minutes.
9. Remove the seeds from the chili, cut it into slices and add it with salt and pepper to the pan.
10. (Be careful not to add too much salt, the anchovies have already released a lot of salt)
11. Once the noodles are cooked, let them drain and dip them in the sauce, mix well and then serve with basil leaves garnish.

Noodles with Pecorino Cheese and Pea Cream

Difficulty level: easy
Preparation: 6 min
Cooking time: 11 min
Servings: 2 people

INGREDIENTS

- 6 oz Noodles (any type)
- 5.5 oz Peas
- 2.5 tablespoon Dried Tomatoes in Oil
- 1.5 tablespoons Extra virgin olive oil
- 1.5 oz Shallot
- 1 tablespoon Pecorino Cheese
- Zest of one Lemon
- Black Pepper
- Salt
- Pecorino Cheese

METHOD

1. Slice the shallot into very thin slices.
2. Add some water to a pot and bring it to a boil for the noodles.
3. In the meantime, heat the oil in a pan and fry the shallot for two minutes on medium heat.
4. Then add the peas, salt, pepper, and a ladle of the pasta cooking water.
5. Cover with a lid and simmer for about 8 minutes.
6. In the meantime, add the noodles to the boiling water and follow the cooking instructions on the package.
7. When the peas are cooked, take three-fourths of them and add them to a high glass, add 1.5 tablespoons olive oil, a ladle of cooking water, and some grated Pecorino cheese.
8. Blend everything with a mixer until a homogenous cream is formed.
9. Add the sun-dried tomatoes to the sauce pot.
10. When the noodles are cooked, drain them and add them to the sauce pot.
11. Now add the pea cream, grated lemon zest and some more Pecorino Cheese on top.

Noodles with Tuna and Ricotta

Difficulty level: very easy
Preparation: 6 min
Cooking time: 11 min
Servings: 2 people

INGREDIENTS

- 6 oz Noodles (any type)
- 2.75 oz Ricotta Cheese
- 2.75 oz Tuna in Oil
- Parsley

METHOD

1. Boil water in a pot. Once it boils, add the water and add the noodles for the cooking time specified on the package.
2. In the meantime, for the topping, drain the tuna in a bowl and mix it with the ricotta cheese.
3. Add two ladles of pasta cooking water and blend with a mixer until creamy and smooth.
4. Wash and chop the parsley.
5. When the noodles are cooked, let them drain and mix them with the ricotta and tuna cream.
6. Sprinkle the dish with parsley before serving.

Rice Plate

Difficulty level: very easy
Preparation: 11 min
Cooking time: 11 min
Servings: 2 people

INGREDIENTS

- 22 tablespoons Cold Saffron Risotto
- 1.5 tablespoons Grana Padano
- Tablespoon of Butter

METHOD

1. Butter a plate, divide the rice into two halves and crush it with a spoon so that two thin slices are formed.
2. Heat a pan and melt a tablespoon of butter, add the risotto to the pan.
3. If the slice breaks, it's no problem, you can put it back together once it's in the pan.
4. Fry the rice on medium heat for 5/6 minutes until it's almost toasted. Then turn it over with a lid, so you can fry the other side, and fry it again for 5/6 minutes.
5. Repeat the process for the other slice and season it with grated Grana Padano before serving.

Noodles with Pesto and Bacon

Difficulty level: easy
Preparation: 11 min
Cooking time: 6 min
Servings: 2 people

INGREDIENTS

- 6 oz Trofie Noodles
- 2 teaspoon Extra virgin olive oil
- 2.75 oz Bacon
- 2 tablespoons Peeled Almonds
- 2 tablespoons Parsley
- 2 tablespoons Extra virgin olive oil
- 1.5 tablespoons Parmesan Cheese
- 1 tablespoon Pine Nuts
- Salt

METHOD

1. Boil a pot of water. Once it boils, salt the water and add the Trofie.
2. Wash the parsley and add the leaves with salt, pine nuts, almonds, and grated Parmesan to a mixer.
3. Add a teaspoon of extra virgin olive oil and mix well. Then stop and add the remaining oil and mix again until smooth.
4. Once you have the sauce ready, you can add the noodles to the boiling water. In the meantime, cut the bacon into about 0.5 inch thick slices and then cut them into cubes.
5. Heat 1.5 tablespoons oil in a pan and fry the bacon for a few minutes. Then add the pesto to the pan, turn off the heat, and stir quickly.
6. Drain the Trofie and add it to the pan with the pesto.

Noodles with Shallot and Salmon

Difficulty level: easy
Preparation: 11 min
Cooking time: 11 min
Servings: 2 people

INGREDIENTS

- 6 oz Penne Noodles
- 5.5 oz Cream
- 3.5 oz Smoked Salmon
- 2.5 oz Tomatoes
- 1.5 tablespoons Extra virgin olive oil
- 1.5 tablespoons Shallot
- Black Pepper
- Salt

METHOD

1. Wash and cut the cherry tomatoes. Chop the shallot and add it to a pan with oil on medium heat for 30 seconds.
2. Cut the salmon into strips and add it to the pan along with the shallots.
3. Also add the cherry tomatoes, salt, pepper, and cream.
4. Boil a pot of water. Once it boils, salt the water and add the noodles.
5. Once the noodles are cooked, drain them and add them to the pan with the sauce.
6. Stir well for a minute, so the dish takes on flavor.

Noodles with Zucchini, Thyme, and Lemon

Difficulty level: very easy
Preparation: 11 min
Servings: 2 people

INGREDIENTS

- 6 oz Noodles (any type)
- 1.5 oz Pecorino cheese
- 3.5 oz Zucchini
- 1 tablespoon Pine nuts
- Zest of 1 Lemon
- Thyme
- Pink Pepper
- 2.5 teaspoons Extra virgin olive oil
- 1.5 tablespoons Lemon juice
- Mustard
- Thyme
- Salt

METHOD

1. Squeeze the lemon until you have about 1.5 tablespoons of juice, and keep it along with oil, salt, mustard, and some thyme leaves in a container. Close the container and shake it for a few seconds.
2. Now boil some water in a pot and add the noodles.
3. You can grate the zucchini while the noodles are cooking. Add the preparation from the container to the zucchini and mix well.
4. Add Pecorino cheese and mix again. Add pine nuts and grated lemon zest and mix again.
5. When the noodles are cooked, drain them and add them to the sauce bowl. Mix for a few minutes until a creamy paste is formed.
6. Before serving, add more thyme, lemon zest, and pink pepper.

Spaghetti Carbonara

Difficulty level: easy
Preparation: 16 min
Cooking time: 11 min
Servings: 2 people

INGREDIENTS

- 6 oz Spaghetti
- Yolks from 3 medium eggs
- 2 tablespoons Pecorino cheese
- 2.75 oz Bacon
- Black Pepper

METHOD

1. Boil some salted water.
2. Meanwhile, cut the bacon into roughly 0.5 inch thick slices and then cut them into cubes.
3. Put the cubes in a pan and fry until crispy (but be careful not to burn them). Once crispy, turn off the heat and remove the pan from the stove to let the bacon cool.
4. In the meantime, add the spaghetti to the boiling water and follow the cooking instructions.
5. In a bowl, mix together the egg yolks, Pecorino cheese, and black pepper. Add a few tablespoons of the pasta cooking water to make the mixture creamier.
6. Once the pasta is cooked, drain it and add it to the pan with the bacon cubes. Pour the egg and Pecorino cream over the top, stir quickly over low heat, do not let the egg become scrambled.
7. Sprinkle with grated Pecorino cheese and black pepper and serve.

Spaghetti with Cheese and Pepper

Difficulty level: easy
Preparation: 11 min
Cooking time: 11 min
Servings: 2 people

INGREDIENTS

- 6 oz Spaghetti
- 3.5 oz Pecorino Romano
- Black pepper
- Salt

METHOD

1. Grate 3.5 oz of Pecorino Romano cheese.
2. Bring a pot of water to a boil, add salt and add the spaghetti to cook.
3. Roast half of the pepper in a pan over low heat and add 1/4 cup of pasta water.
4. Drain the spaghetti two minutes before the time indicated on the package and add it to the pan with the roasted pepper. (Keep the pasta water.)
5. Cook the spaghetti like rice, continuing to cook and adding more water as needed (when all the water in the pan has evaporated).
6. Then continue with the cheese cream, add about 1.7 oz of cheese in a bowl, add some pasta water, stir and add more pasta water if needed.
7. Add the remaining 1.7 oz of Pecorino cheese with some water and stir until the cream is smooth and homogeneous.
8. Add the cheese cream to the spaghetti and mix everything very quickly by continuing to toss and move the spaghetti.
9. Serve with black pepper and grated Pecorino cheese, if desired.

Noodles with Guanciale and Pecorino Cheese

Difficulty level: easy
Preparation: 11 min
Cooking time: 16 min
Servings: 2 people

INGREDIENTS

- 6 oz Rigatoni noodles
- 2 tablespoons grated Pecorino Romano cheese
- 4.5 oz Guanciale
- Salt

METHOD

1. Boil a pot of water for the noodles.
2. Cut the bacon into 0.5 inch thick slices, then cut it again into cubes.
3. Add the Guanciale to a pan and cook it on medium heat for about 10 minutes, or until the cubes are crispy, but be careful not to burn them.
4. In the meantime, the water should be boiling, so add salt and put the noodles in.
5. Grate the Pecorino cheese into very fine flakes.
6. Add a scoop of the pasta water to the Guanciale and cook on medium heat, so that a creamy mixture forms with the Guanciale.
7. When the noodles are cooked, drain them and add them to the pan with the Guanciale. Cook for a few minutes while stirring, then remove the pan from the heat and add the grated Pecorino cheese. Stir and toss again, so that the Pecorino melts and a creamy texture is created.
8. Sprinkle with grated Pecorino cheese and serve.

Penne with Cream and Ham

Difficulty level: easy
Preparation: min6
Cooking time: 13 min
Servings: 2 people

INGREDIENTS

- 6 oz Penne noodles
- 5.5 oz cream
- 1 tablespoon tomato paste
- 2 oz sliced cooked ham
- Extra virgin olive oil
- Parsley
- Black pepper
- Salt

METHOD

1. Wash, dry and finely chop the parsley. Slice the cooked ham into thin strips.
2. Boil a pot of water, salt the water.
3. In a pan, cook the ham with some oil for 1 minute, then add in the cream.
4. Mix well and then add in the tomato paste, cook for 9 minutes on low heat.
5. When the water boils, drop in the noodles and cook for the time specified on the package.
6. Once the noodles are cooked, drain them and add them to the sauce, season with salt and pepper, mix everything together and add in the parsley.

Noodles with Zucchini

Difficulty level: very easy
Preparation: 6 min
Cooking time: 14 min
Servings: 2 people

INGREDIENTS

- 6 oz Noodles (any type)
- 11.5 oz Zucchini
- 2 teaspoon extra virgin olive oil
- 1 garlic clove
- Basil
- Black pepper
- Salt

METHOD

1. Boil a pot of water. Once it boils, salt the water and add the noodles.
2. Wash and dry the zucchini, remove the ends and grate them into large pieces. Clean a garlic clove and heat it with oil in a pan.
3. Once the oil is hot, add the zucchini, season with salt and pepper and sauté for about 5 minutes.
4. When the noodles are cooked, drain and add them to the saucepan.
5. Mix well and serve with some basil.

Spinach Spätzle with Bacon and Cream

Difficulty level: easy
Preparation: 14 min
Cooking time: 16 min
Servings: 2 people

INGREDIENTS

- 1 1/4 cup all-purpose flour
- 5 oz spinach
- 1/4 cup water
- 1 large egg
- Nutmeg for grating
- Salt
- 1/2 cup heavy cream
- 1 1/2 tbsp butter
- 2 oz bacon
- 2 tbsp chives
- Extra-virgin olive oil
- Black pepper
- Salt

METHOD

1. Wash the spinach and cook it in a pan over medium heat, cover it with a lid and cook until the spinach has wilted. Puree the spinach in a blender until smooth. Add the whole egg with some salt. Stir everything for a few minutes and then add the water and some nutmeg. Slowly pour in the flour while stirring constantly to avoid clumps.
2. Slice the bacon and chop the chives. Heat butter and oil in a frying pan. Once hot, add the bacon and cook for a few minutes (or until crispy). Add the cream, salt, pepper, and chives and cook over medium heat until creamy.
3. Now cook the Spätzle: Bring a pot of salted water to a boil. When the water is boiling, use a Spätzle press and drop the mixture into the water, so that everything falls in. The Spätzle will be done in just a few seconds.
4. Once the Spätzle float to the surface, drain them and add them to the pan with the cream and bacon. Mix everything for about 30 seconds while stirring constantly and season with pepper and salt.

Creamy Pasta with Pepper Flavor

Difficulty level: easy
Preparation: 6 min
Cooking time: 14 min
Servings: 2 people

INGREDIENTS

- 7 oz red bell pepper
- 6 oz Penne pasta
- 4.5 oz Auburn tomatoes
- Extra virgin olive oil
- Basil
- 1 garlic clove
- Black pepper
- Salt

METHOD

1. Boil a pot of water.
2. Wash the pepper, cut off the top and then cut it in half so you can remove the seeds inside. Then cut the pepper into cubes.
3. Cut the tomato into large pieces. Saute the garlic in a pan with a little oil for about 1 minute. Then add the pepper, tomatoes, salt, pepper, and basil. Cook for 14 minutes.
4. Once the water is boiling, add salt and the pasta and cook for the time indicated on the package.
5. Put the contents of the pot with the tomatoes and pepper into a high container and puree it with a mixer. Once it is creamy, pour it back into the previously used pan and let it heat up on very low heat.
6. Once the pasta is cooked, drain it and add it to the sauce, mix everything well and serve with some basil.

Noodles with Onions and Salmon

Difficulty level: very easy
Preparation: 11 min
Cooking time: 21 min
Servings: 2 people

INGREDIENTS

- 7 oz Räucherlachs
- 6 oz Tagliatelle-Noodles
- 3.5 oz Cream
- Extra virgin olive oil
- Parsley
- 1/2 Onions
- Black pepper

METHOD

1. Boil a pot of water and salt the water once it is boiling.
2. Chop salmon, onion, and parsley.
3. Sauté the onion for 30 seconds in a pan with hot oil, then add in the salmon and turn the heat high. Sauté for about 2 minutes.
4. Once the water is boiling, you can add in the noodles and cook for the time specified on the package. In the meantime, add in the cream to the pan with the salmon (without increasing the heat).
5. Once the noodles are cooked, drain them and add them to the sauce pot. Turn on the heat and stir well so that all ingredients combine.
6. Before serving, add in chopped parsley and some pepper.

Risotto with Parmesan Cheese

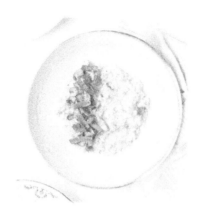

Difficulty level: easy
Preparation: 6 min
Cooking time: 26 min
Servings: 2 people

INGREDIENTS

- 7 oz Carnaroli Rice
- 2 oz Parmesan cheese
- 3 cups beef broth
- 1 tsp extra virgin olive oil
- 3 tablespoons onions
- 2 tbsp butter
- Salt

METHOD

1. Finely chop the onion. Melt 2 tbsp of butter in a pan and then add the onion and 1 tsp of oil. Cook on low heat until the onions are soft.
2. Now add the rice and roast for 2 minutes on high heat, then add 1/4 cup of hot beef broth and stir constantly. Once the broth is absorbed, add another 1/4 cup. Continue until the rice is cooked.
3. Add the last 10 g (2 tsp) of butter and grated Parmesan, stir and mix well.

Noodles with Ricotta

Difficulty level: very easy
Preparation: 11 min
Cooking time: 16 min
Servings: 2 people

INGREDIENTS

- 6 oz pasta (any kind)
- 2.5 tablespoon cream
- 2.5 tablespoon grated parmesan cheese
- 6.25 oz Ricotta
- Thyme
- Black pepper
- Salt

METHOD

1. Boil a pot of water. Once it boils, salt the water and add the pasta.
2. Strain the Ricotta through a sieve to remove any lumps and achieve a smooth Ricotta.
3. Add fresh cream and grated parmesan cheese and mix everything together. Then add thyme leaves along with salt and pepper and mix again.
4. When the pasta is cooked, drain it and add it to the Ricotta sauce, mixing everything thoroughly.

Noodles with Gorgonzola and Olives

Difficulty level: very easy
Preparation: 16 min
Cooking time: 11 min
Servings: 2 people

INGREDIENTS

- 6 oz Rigatoni pasta
- 2.25 oz cream
- 3.25 oz Gorgonzola cheese
- 1.5 tablespoons Black olives (pitted)
- Black pepper
- Salt

METHOD

1. Purée the olives in a blender.
2. Boil a pot of water. Once it boils, salt the water and add the pasta.
3. Meanwhile, cut the Gorgonzola cheese into cubes and add it along with the cream in a pot. Melt it over low heat, stirring frequently to promote melting.
4. Drain the pasta 1 minute before the time indicated on the package. Once it is drained, add it along with the Gorgonzola in the pan and finish cooking it while stirring and mixing everything together. After a minute, add the puréed olives in the pan and stir again.

Noodles with Tuna

Difficulty level: easy
Preparation: 11 min
Cooking time: 16 min
Servings: 2 people

INGREDIENTS

- 6 oz pasta (any kind)
- 7 oz canned crushed tomatoes
- 4.5 oz canned tuna in oil
- 1.5 tablespoons extra virgin olive oil
- 1.5 teaspoon canned anchovies in oil
- 1 sprig of parsley for chopping
- 1 fresh chili pepper
- 1 garlic clove
- Salt

METHOD

1. Boil a pot of water. Once it boils, salt the water and add the pasta.
2. Cook the garlic in a pan with some oil for 15 seconds. Then remove it.
3. Add anchovy fillets and a bit of water from the pasta cooking time to the pan and let the fillets dissolve.
4. Then slice the chili pepper thinly and add it to the pan. Drain the tuna from the oil and add it to the pan.
5. Add more pasta cooking water and canned crushed tomatoes and let it cook for 10 minutes.
6. Once the pasta is cooked, drain it and add it to the sauce pot.
7. Stir to mix everything together, add salt, pepper and chopped parsley.

Noodles with Gorgonzola and Walnuts

Difficulty level: very easy
Preparation: 11 min
Cooking time: 16 min
Servings: 2 people

INGREDIENTS

- 6.25 oz Gorgonzola
- 6 oz Noodles (any type)
- 2.75 oz Cream
- 1.75 oz Walnuts
- Black pepper
- Thyme
- Salt

METHOD

1. Boil a pot of water. Once it boils, salt the water and add the noodles.
2. Heat the cream on low flame, cut the Gorgonzola into cubes and add it to the pan with the cream. Add pepper and some thyme and cook for a few minutes on low flame.
3. Chop the inside of the nuts.
4. Once the noodles are cooked, drain them and add them to the pan with the sauce.
5. Mix everything well and then add the chopped walnuts, stir again and it's ready to serve.

Noodles with Zucchini and Eggs

Difficulty level: very easy
Preparation: 11 min
Cooking time: 16 min
Servings: 2 people

INGREDIENTS

- 6 oz Noodles (any type)
- 3.5 oz Zucchini
- 2 egg yolks
- 1.75 oz Pecorino cheese (grated)
- Extra virgin olive oil
- Salt
- Black pepper

METHOD

1. Wash the zucchini and cut off the ends, then cut it into sticks and dice it.
2. Boil a pot of water. Once it boils, salt the water and add the noodles.
3. Heat the oil in a pan. Once it's hot, add the zucchini and sauté for 7 minutes on high heat, so it becomes crispy.
4. Mix the egg yolks with the sheep's cheese in a separate bowl and add a little cooking water to make a creamy mixture.
5. Once the noodles are cooked, drain them and add them to the pan with the zucchini. Then add the egg yolk-cheese mixture with the heat off.
6. Mix everything together and serve it sprinkled with the Pecorino cheese.

Noodles with Red Pesto

Difficulty level: very easy
Preparation: 16 min
Cooking time: 11 min
Servings: 2 people

INGREDIENTS

- 6 oz Rigatoni noodles
- 2 teaspoon peeled almonds
- 1 tablespoon pine nuts
- 7 oz dried tomatoes in oil
- 5 basil leaves

METHOD

1. In a blender, put: sun-dried tomatoes (without draining the oil), pine nuts, peeled almonds and basil leaves. Pulse everything until a grainy mixture is formed.
2. Boil a pot of water. Once it boils, salt the water and add the noodles.
3. Set aside about 4.6 oz of the cooking water.
4. Drain the noodles two minutes before the time indicated on the package. Add the grainy mixture to the pot where the water was boiled. Add 4.6 oz of cooking water to make a delicious cream.
5. Mix well and add the noodles to the pot. Stir for 2 minutes over low heat to finish cooking the noodles.

Salmon Risotto

Difficulty level: easy
Preparation: 16 min
Cooking time: 16 min
Servings: 2 people

INGREDIENTS

- 6.25 oz Carnaroli rice
- 9 oz fish stock
- 4.5 oz salmon fillet
- Extra virgin olive oil
- 2 teaspoon Grana Padano cheese
- 1 leek
- 1 garlic clove
- Black pepper
- Salt
- 1.5 oz butter
- 1 sprig of thyme
- 1 sprig of dill
- 1 bunch of marjoram
- Zest of half a lemon
- Salt

METHOD

1. Chop the herbs (thyme, dill, marjoram) and grate the lemon zest. Melt the butter at room temperature until creamy, then add the herbs, lemon zest and salt.
2. Clean the salmon and cut it into small pieces.
3. Cook the salmon for a few minutes with a garlic clove in a pan with a tablespoon of oil, season it and remove the garlic at the end of 2 minutes.
4. Finely chop the leek and cook it on low heat in a pan with two tablespoons of oil until it wilts.
5. Roast the rice on high heat in the pan while stirring constantly.
6. When the salmon is cooked, add the salmon cubes, salt, herb butter and some Grana Padano cheese.

Crispy Spaghetti with Sardines

Difficulty level: very easy
Preparation: 6 min
Cooking time: 26 min
Servings: 2 people

INGREDIENTS

- 6 oz Spaghetti
- 1 tablespoon Sardines in oil
- 2 teaspoon extra virgin olive oil
- 2.5 tablespoon breadcrumbs
- 2 garlic cloves

METHOD

1. Boil a pot of water. Once the water boils, dip the pasta in.
2. Dissolve the sardines (after draining them from the oil) in a pan with 2 ⅔ tablespoon of oil, the two whole garlic cloves and some cooking water.
3. Stir constantly for about 10 minutes.
4. Add another 2 ⅔ tablespoon of oil to another pan and add the breadcrumbs and fry until golden brown.
5. Cook the spaghetti 1 minute less than indicated on the package. Then remove the garlic from the pan, drain the pasta and add it to the pan.
6. Cook the pasta in the pan until done, then stir for a generous minute and mix everything together.
7. When they are done, turn off the heat, add most of the breadcrumbs and stir again.
8. Finally, sprinkle with the breadcrumbs and serve.

Noodles with Lemon and Tuna

Difficulty level: very easy
Preparation: 16 min
Cooking time: 16 min
Servings: 2 people

INGREDIENTS

- 6 oz Noodles (any type)
- 5.75 oz Tuna in oil
- 1 tablespoon shallot
- 1 tablespoon lemon juice
- 1 fresh chili
- Zest of one lemon
- Extra virgin olive oil
- Black pepper

Salt

METHOD

1. Drain the oil from the tuna.
2. Boil a pot of water. Once it boils, salt the water and add the noodles.
3. Wash the lemon, dry it and zest it. Then cut it in half and squeeze it. You get about 2 tablespoons of juice.
4. Slice the shallot thinly and sauté it on low heat in a pan with oil. Add a little cooking water and cook for about 6 minutes.
5. Slice the chili, remove the seeds and add it to the pan. Also add the lemon zest and more cooking water. Add the drained tuna and lemon juice, raise the heat and cook for 2 minutes then lower the temperature.
6. Once the noodles are cooked, drain them and add them to the pan. Mix everything well together.

Noodles with Radicchio and Bacon

Difficulty level: very easy
Preparation: 11 min
Cooking time: 21 min
Servings: 2 people

INGREDIENTS

- 6 oz Noodles (any type)
- 1.75 oz Cream
- 3.25 oz Bacon
- 7 oz Radicchio
- 1 tablespoon Shallot
- 1 tablespoon Extra virgin olive oil
- 2 tablespoons Tomato paste
- Black pepper
- Salt

METHOD

1. Finely chop the shallot. Cut the bacon into equal sized sticks. Clean the radicchio and remove the outer leaves. Halve them lengthwise, remove the stem and cut everything into thin strips.
2. Cook the shallots on low heat for 5 minutes in a pan with oil. Then add the bacon and cook for another 4 minutes. Then add the liquid cream and tomato paste. Add salt and pepper and cook for another 6 minutes.
3. Meanwhile, cook the noodles in a pot of salted water. 2 minutes before the time indicated on the package, drain the noodles. Finish cooking in the pan with the spices.
4. Then drain 2 minutes before and add the noodles, stirring for 2 minutes in the sauce.
5. When it's cooked, add the radicchio and mix everything again.

Spaghetti with Spinach and Ricotta

Difficulty level: very easy
Preparation: 11 min
Cooking time: 16 min
Servings: 2 people

INGREDIENTS

- 8 oz Spaghetti
- 5.5 oz Ricotta Cheese
- 1 pinch Nutmeg
- 1 tablespoon Olive Oil
- 7 oz Spinach
- 2 oz Grana Padano Cheese
- 1 Garlic clove
- Black pepper
- Salt

METHOD

1. Bring a pot of water to a boil, add salt and spaghetti.
2. Wash and dry the spinach.
3. In a pan, sauté garlic for 1 minute in olive oil.
4. Add the spinach to the pan, cover with a lid and cook for 3 minutes.
5. Remove the garlic and puree the spinach in a blender until smooth.
6. In a separate pot, heat the spinach puree and ricotta cheese over low heat, stirring occasionally, and add a little pasta water if needed. Cook for about 5 minutes, then season with salt and pepper.
7. Drain the spaghetti and add it to the pot with the sauce. Add a little more pasta water if needed, and stir well to combine. Serve with grated grana padano cheese.

Fettuccine with Truffles

Difficulty level: easy
Preparation: 15 min
Cooking time: 15 min
Servings: 4 people

INGREDIENTS

- 4.5 Oz Fettuccine
- 2 tablespoons Extra Virgin Olive Oil
- 1.5 tablespoons Butter
- 1.5 Oz black Truffle
- 1 Garlic clove
- Salt

METHOD

1. Wash the truffle carefully with cold water, to remove the dirt, then clean it with a brush, rinse it and dry it.
2. Slice the truffle very thinly.
3. Heat the oil and butter in a frying pan over low heat.
4. Clean the garlic clove and add it to the pan with oil and butter for a few minutes. Then remove it, turn off the heat and add the truffle. (Leave some slices for decoration before serving.)
5. Stir the contents of the pan with the heat off.
6. In the meantime, bring a pot of water to a boil. Once it boils, add the water and submerge the fettuccine.
7. Drain the fettuccine and add it to the sauce pot, stir well so that everything is mixed.
8. Serve with the decoration of slices left from the previous steps.

Noodles with Gorgonzola

Difficulty level: very easy
Preparation: 11 min
Cooking time: 21 min
Servings: 2 people

INGREDIENTS

- 8 oz Penne pasta
- 3/4 cup heavy cream
- 6 oz Gorgonzola cheese
- Black pepper
- Salt

METHOD

1. Cut the Gorgonzola cheese into cubes and place them in a pot with the heavy cream. Season with pepper.
2. Cook on low heat for about 10 minutes, or until the cheese is melted and the sauce is smooth.
3. Bring a pot of salted water to a boil, and add the pasta. Cook according to package instructions until al dente.
4. Drain the pasta and add it to the pot with the sauce.
5. Keep the heat low and stir everything together. After about 1 minute, you can serve the pasta with Gorgonzola.

Champagne-Risotto

Difficulty level: very easy
Preparation: 6 min
Cooking time: 21 min
Servings: 2 people

INGREDIENTS

- 7 oz Carnaroli rice
- 9.25 oz Champagne
- 9.25 oz Vegetable broth
- 1.75 oz Parmesan cheese
- 2 tablespoons Butter
- 1 small onion

METHOD

1. Finely chop the onion.
2. Add 1 tablespoon of butter to a pan and add the onion, heat until browned.
3. Add the rice to the pan and roast for 5 seconds on high heat.
4. Pour in the champagne and stir constantly to prevent the rice from sticking to the pan.
5. Add some vegetable broth to cook the rice.
6. When the rice is cooked (or a few seconds before), turn off the heat and melt the remaining tablespoon of butter in the pan and stir again to combine.

Farmer's Pasta

Difficulty level: very easy
Preparation: 16 min
Cooking time: 9 min
Servings: 3 people

INGREDIENTS

- 9 oz Spaghetti
- 3.5 oz Pecorino cheese
- Extra virgin olive oil
- 1 clove of garlic
- 1 fresh chili pepper
- 1 sprig of parsley
- Salt

METHOD

1. Bring a pot of water to a boil, add salt, and add the pasta.
2. Chop the fresh chili pepper and parsley.
3. Peel and chop the garlic and grate the Pecorino cheese.
4. In a bowl, add the garlic, chopped chili pepper, olive oil, and salt, mix well.
5. Once the pasta is cooked, drain it and add it to the bowl with the sauce.
6. Stir and serve topped with grated Pecorino cheese.

Curry-Rice

Difficulty level: easy
Preparation: 11 min
Cooking time: 21 min
Servings: 2 people

INGREDIENTS

- 5.75 oz Basmati Rice
- 6.25 oz Water
- 3.25 oz Peas
- 4 oz Leek
- 2 small fresh chili peppers
- 1 teaspoon Curry powder
- Extra virgin olive oil
- Salt

METHOD

1. Rinse the rice and place it in a pot with salt and water. Cover with a lid and bring the water to a boil.
2. Once it reaches a boil, lower the heat to low and cook for an additional 7 minutes.
3. Meanwhile, chop the chili peppers and slice the leek.
4. After 7 minutes, the rice should be cooked, remove it from the heat and let it rest for 11 minutes.
5. Take a pan and add oil, leek, and chili pepper and cook on low heat for about 5 minutes.
6. Add curry powder and peas and stir well for about 3 minutes on medium heat, adding salt as needed.
7. Add the rice to the pan and stir on low heat for a few minutes.

Noodles with Cherry Tomatoes and Cream Cheese

Difficulty level: very easy
Preparation: 11 min
Cooking time: 16 min
Servings: 2 people

INGREDIENTS

- 5.75 oz pasta (any type)
- 4.25 oz cream cheese
- 5.5 oz cherry tomatoes
- 2 tablespoons extra virgin olive oil
- 1 teaspoon brown sugar
- Oregano
- 1 clove of garlic
- Black pepper
- Salt

METHOD

1. Boil a pot of water. Once it is boiling, add salt to the water and add the pasta.
2. In a mixing bowl, add two-thirds of the cream cheese, salt, pepper, fresh oregano, and 2 teaspoons of olive oil. Wash and dry half of the cherry tomatoes and add them to the bowl.
3. Mix the ingredients until it forms a homogenous cream.
4. Cut the remaining cherry tomatoes in half.
5. Heat a frying pan with olive oil and the peeled garlic clove for 30 seconds, then add the brown sugar and halved cherry tomatoes and cook for 2 minutes on high heat, then remove the garlic from the pan.
6. Once the pasta is cooked, drain it, put it in the sauce pot and add the cream cheese mixture.
7. Stir on low heat and add fresh oregano leaves.

Penne with Sausage

Difficulty level: very easy
Preparation: 6 min
Cooking time: 16 min
Servings: 2 people

INGREDIENTS

- 6 oz Penne pasta
- 4.5 oz Cream
- 4.5 oz Sausage
- 2 tablespoons Parmesan cheese
- Black pepper
- Salt

METHOD

1. Boil a pot of water. Once it is boiling, salt the water and add the pasta.
2. Remove the skin from the sausage and cut it into 1/4 inch pieces.
3. Fry the pieces in a pan until they are golden brown and almost crispy.
4. Add the cream, pepper and salt, and cook for 10 minutes.
5. When the pasta is cooked, drain it and add it to the pan with the sauce, stirring well to combine all the flavors.
6. Turn off the heat and add the grated parmesan cheese.
7. Taste and adjust seasoning with salt and pepper.

Mountain-Risotto

Difficulty level: easy
Preparation: 11 min
Cooking time: 21 min
Servings: 2 people

INGREDIENTS

- 6 oz Carnaroli rice
- 2.25 cups Vegetable broth
- 2 oz Ricotta
- 2.75 oz Bacon
- 1 tablespoon Butter
- 1 tablespoon Chopped parsley
- 1 small Onion
- Black pepper
- Salt

METHOD

1. Finely chop the onion and parsley.
2. Cut the bacon into small cubes.
3. Melt the butter in a pan, add the onion, and cook for 10 minutes. Then add the bacon cubes and mix well.
4. Add the rice to the pan and cook until it becomes translucent. Then add the vegetable broth gradually, stirring occasionally, until it is absorbed.
5. Once the rice is cooked, add the ricotta and stir until it melts and combine with the other ingredients.
6. Serve with chopped parsley on top.

Neapolitan Pasta

Difficulty level: easy
Preparation: 6 min
Cooking time: 21 min
Servings: 2 people

INGREDIENTS

- 6 oz Spaghetti
- 7 oz Peeled tomatoes
- 2 oz Mozzarella
- 1.5 tablespoons Stoned black olives
- 1 tablespoon Salted capers
- 2.5 tablespoon Red onions
- 0.2 tablespoons Fresh chili
- Extra virgin olive oil
- Fresh Oregano
- Salt

METHOD

1. Clean and slice the red onions and chili, and slice the olives in the same way. Drain the mozzarella and cut it into small pieces.
2. Boil a pot of water. Once it is boiling, salt the water and add the pasta.
3. Put the onions and chili in a pan with olive oil. Cook over medium heat until the onions are golden brown, add 2 tablespoons of pasta water as needed.
4. Add the tomatoes to the pan and mash them with a wooden spoon. Add the olives, capers and salt. Cook on low heat. After 12 minutes add the mozzarella pieces and oregano.
5. When the pasta is cooked, drain it and add it to the pan with the sauce, stirring well to combine all the ingredients.

Pasta with Peas and Tuna

Difficulty level: easy
Preparation: 6 min
Cooking time: 21 min
Servings: 2 people

INGREDIENTS

- 6 oz Spaghetti
- 3.25 oz Cherry tomatoes
- 3 oz Peas
- 2.5 oz Drained Tuna in oil
- 1 Garlic clove
- Extra virgin olive oil
- Basil
- Black pepper
- Salt

METHOD

1. Boil a pot of water. Once it is boiling, salt the water and add the pasta.
2. Wash and halve the cherry tomatoes.
3. Heat a pan with oil and sauté the peeled garlic for 15 seconds.
4. Add the cherry tomatoes and when they begin to release their juice, add the peas and cook for 4 to 5 minutes.
5. Add the basil and continue to cook the sauce over medium heat for another 4 to 5 minutes.
6. Remove the garlic from the sauce, add the drained tuna and let the sauce cook for a few more minutes. (If it's too dry, add more pasta water.)
7. Drain the pasta 2 minutes before the end of cooking time and add it to the sauce pot.
8. Salt and pepper the mixture and stir for a few minutes.

Pasta with Creamy Broccoli

Difficulty level: very easy
Preparation: 16 min
Cooking time: 16 min
Servings: 2 people

INGREDIENTS

- 6 oz Pasta (any kind)
- Salt
- 6 oz Broccoli
- 2.5 tablespoon Extra virgin olive oil
- 1 tablespoon Grana Padano cheese
- 1 tablespoon Pine nuts
- 1.5 teaspoon Basil
- 1.5 teaspoon Peeled almonds
- Salt

METHOD

1. Wash the broccoli and separate the florets. Boil a pot of water, blanch the florets for 5 minutes, then drain and cool them in a bowl of cold water.
2. Once cooled, dry and place the florets, peeled almonds, grated Grana Padano cheese, basil leaves, pine nuts, salt and 1.2 tablespoon of olive oil in a blender. Blend the ingredients for a few seconds, then add the remaining olive oil and blend again. You should have a homogeneous cream, if it's too dry, add more oil.
3. Boil a pot of water. Once it is boiling, salt the water and add the pasta.
4. Add the broccoli cream along with a ladle of pasta water in a pot and heat it slightly on low heat.
5. When the pasta is cooked, drain it and add it to the pan with the sauce, keeping the heat low and stir for about a minute.

Pasta with Breadcrumbs

Difficulty level: easy
Preparation: 11 min
Cooking time: 11 min
Servings: 2 people

INGREDIENTS

- 6 oz Spaghetti
- 2 oz Breadcrumbs
- 1.75 oz Extra virgin olive oil
- 2 Salted anchovy fillets
- 1 Hot chili pepper
- 1 sprig Parsley
- 1 Garlic clove
- Salt

METHOD

1. Use a blender to finely chop the breadcrumbs. Finely chop the parsley and chili pepper with a knife (remove the inner seeds).
2. Boil a pot of water. Once it is boiling, salt the water and add the pasta.
3. Heat 25 ml oil in a pan over low heat with half a garlic clove. After 30/40 seconds add the breadcrumbs and stir constantly to avoid burning. Cook for about 6 minutes over medium heat.
4. Heat another pan with the remaining 25 ml of oil, add the chili and the other half of the garlic clove.
5. Drain the oil from the anchovy fillets and add them to the pan, to melt them over medium heat.
6. When the spaghetti is cooked, drain it and add it to the pan with the anchovies.
7. Mix the pasta with the sauce and then add the toasted breadcrumbs and chopped parsley.

Pasta with Cream and Onions

Difficulty level: easy
Preparation: 11 min
Cooking time: 19 min
Servings: 2 people

INGREDIENTS

- 6 oz Penne Pasta
- 2.75 oz Cream
- 7 oz Passata (pureed tomatoes)
- 1.5 oz diced bacon
- 1 red onion
- 1 tablespoon Extra virgin olive oil
- Basil
- Salt

METHOD

1. Slice the onion finely. Heat a pan with a tablespoon of olive oil and add the bacon and onion, sauté on high flame for 3 minutes.
2. Add the passata and salt, mix the ingredients and cook for 15 minutes over medium heat.
3. Boil a pot of water. Once it is boiling, salt the water and add the pasta.
4. Add the cream to the sauce and stir everything together.
5. Once the pasta is cooked, drain it and add it to the sauce pot. Stir well.
6. Serve with basil leaves.

Lime Pasta

Difficulty level: very easy
Preparation: 11 min
Cooking time: 16 min
Servings: 2 people

INGREDIENTS

- 6 oz Pasta
- 4.5 oz Mascarpone
- 2 tablespoons Grana Padano
- 1 Lime
- Pink pepper

METHOD

1. Boil a pot of water. Once it is boiling, salt the water and add the pasta. Place the Mascarpone in a pan and season with salt and pepper (you don't need to turn on the heat). Wash the Lime and squeeze its juice into the Mascarpone bowl. Stir.
2. Once the pasta is cooked, drain it and add it to the sauce pot (save some of the pasta water). Add a ladle of the pasta water and stir constantly. The Mascarpone will melt and form a cream due to the heat of the water.
3. Add pink pepper and finely grated lime zest. Stir again. Serve with grated Grana Padano cheese on top.

Gnocchi with Pea Cream

Difficulty level: easy
Preparation: 11 min
Cooking time: 21 min
Servings: 2 people

INGREDIENTS

- 7 oz Gnocchi
- 8 oz Peas
- 1/2 oz Pecorino cheese
- 1/2 oz Grana Padano cheese
- 1/2 oz Shallot
- 1/2 oz Butter
- Vegetable broth
- Nutmeg
- Salt

METHOD

1. Finely chop the shallot and sauté in a pan with butter for a few minutes. Then add the peas and cook for 15 minutes (or until they are soft). If necessary, add vegetable broth.
2. Once they are cooked, transfer the peas to a blender and puree until they form a smooth cream.
3. Transfer the cream to another pot, add nutmeg, white pepper, Pecorino cheese, and Grana Padano cheese, and stir well.
4. Boil a pot of water, when it boils, salt the water and add the gnocchi.
5. When the Gnocchi is cooked, drain them and add them to the sauce pan, stirring quickly to mix everything.

Cold Pasta with Cherry Tomatoes and Ricotta Cheese

Difficulty level: easy
Preparation: 16 min
Cooking time: 16 min
Servings: 2 people

INGREDIENTS

- 8 oz Noodles (any type)
- 8 oz Cherry tomatoes
- 4 oz Tomatoes
- 4 oz Aged cheese
- 4 oz Buffalo ricotta
- 2 tablespoons Pitted olives
- 1 tbsp Extra virgin olive oil
- 1 tablespoon Basil
- 1 tbsp Parmesan cheese
- Black pepper
- Salt

METHOD

1. Boil a pot of water. Once it boils, add salt and noodles.
2. Blend in a blender: Cherry tomatoes, basil, parmesan, basil, oil, salt, and pepper. You should get a homogeneous cream.
3. Pour the cream in a large bowl, it will be used to plate the pasta.
4. Cut the aged cheese into small cubes. Now, wash the tomatoes and cut them into cubes.
5. Once the noodles are cooked, drain them and cool them under cold water. Then add the noodles to the bowl with the sauce. Add the aged cheese and olives to the bowl. Mix everything together.

Spaghetti with Sardines, sun-dried Tomatoes, and Crispy Breadcrumbs

Difficulty level: very easy
Preparation: 16 min
Cooking time: 11 min
Servings: 2 people

INGREDIENTS

- 8 Oz Spaghetti
- 1.5 Oz Dried Tomatoes
- 1 tablespoon Sardines In Oil
- 3 Tablespoons Extra Virgin Olive Oil
- 1 Fresh Chili Pepper
- 1 Clove Garlic
- Breadcrumbs
- Salt

METHOD

1. Cook a pot of water and add the spaghetti.
2. Soak the sun-dried tomatoes in a bowl of very hot water for 15 minutes.
3. Drain the sardines and finely chop them, also chop the chili pepper (removing the seeds) and garlic.
4. Heat 1.5 tablespoons of olive oil in a pan and add the sardines, garlic, and chili pepper on low heat.
5. After 15 minutes, drain the tomatoes and pat them dry. Cut them into thin strips and add them to the sauce pan.
6. In another pan, heat 1.5 tablespoons of olive oil and fry the breadcrumbs until crispy.
7. When the spaghetti is cooked, drain it and add it to the sauce pan. Mix well.
8. Serve with crispy breadcrumbs on top.

Linguine with Pesto

Difficulty level: easy
Preparation: 11 min
Cooking time: 11 min
Servings: 2 people

INGREDIENTS

- 8 oz Linguine pasta
- 1.75 oz extra-virgin olive oil
- 2.5 tablespoon grated Parmesan cheese
- 1 tablespoon Pecorino cheese
- 2 tablespoons basil leaves
- 1.5 teaspoon pine nuts
- 1/2 clove of garlic
- Coarse salt
- Basil leaves

METHOD

1. Add the peeled garlic and coarse salt to a food processor and pulse until creamy. Add the basil leaves and pulse again. Then add the pine nuts, Parmesan and Pecorino cheese and blend all ingredients together, gradually adding the extra-virgin olive oil. The end result should be a homogenous cream.
2. Boil a pot of water and add coarse salt. Add the pasta and cook according to package instructions.
3. Pour the pesto in a pan and add a few tablespoons of pasta water (turn off the heat). Stir to combine the water with the pesto sauce.
4. Once pasta is cooked, drain it and add it to the pesto pan, toss well and serve with a few basil leaves on top.

Spaghetti Carbonara (Version with Fish)

Difficulty level: easy
Preparation: 11 min
Cooking time: 16 min
Servings: 2 people

INGREDIENTS

- 8 oz spaghetti
- 5.5 oz salmon fillet
- 2 tablespoons Pecorino cheese
- 2 egg yolks (from small eggs)
- 1 egg (small)
- Extra virgin olive oil
- 1 garlic clove
- Black pepper
- Salt

METHOD

1. Boil a pot of water. Once it boils, salt the water and add the spaghetti. Cut the salmon into about 0.75 inch cubes.
2. Heat the oil with the garlic clove in a pan, add the salmon and cook for a few minutes. Season with salt and remove the garlic from the pan.
3. In a bowl, beat the egg and the two egg yolks. Then add the grated Pecorino cheese and pepper and stir again to mix everything.
4. When the spaghetti is cooked, drain and add it to the sauce pan, keep a medium flame and stir. Now turn down the heat and add the cheese-egg mixture, stirring everything very quickly. Serve with a final pinch of pepper.

Pumpkin-Gnocchi

Difficulty level: easy
Preparation: 16 min
Cooking time: 6 min
Servings: 2 people

INGREDIENTS

- 1 lb pumpkin
- 1 egg
- 1/2 cup all-purpose flour
- 2 tablespoons grated Parmesan cheese
- 1 clove of garlic
- 1/4 cup Ricotta cheese
- Rosemary
- Salt
- 2 tablespoons butter
- 1 sprig of rosemary

METHOD

1. Cut the pumpkin in half, remove the seeds and skin. Then cut it into slices.
2. Place the pumpkin, garlic, and rosemary in a microwave-safe bowl. Cover with plastic wrap. Cook in the microwave for about 7 minutes, until the pumpkin is soft.
3. In another bowl, mix together the Ricotta cheese, egg, and grated Parmesan.
4. Use a potato masher to mash the pumpkin. Add the mashed pumpkin to the bowl with the Ricotta mixture. Add the flour and salt to the bowl and mix everything together.
5. Fill a pastry bag with the pumpkin mixture.
6. Heat a pan over medium heat and melt the butter with the rosemary until the butter is browned.
7. Bring a pot of salted water to a boil. Use the pastry bag to form the pumpkin dumplings and drop them into the boiling water.
8. When the gnocchi are cooked, drain them and add them to the pan with the butter and rosemary. Stir briefly to coat them in the butter.

Penne with Ham, Cream and Peas

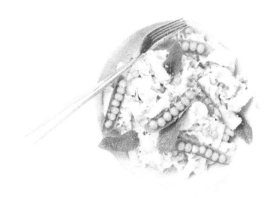

Difficulty level: easy
Preparation: 6 min
Cooking time: 21 min
Servings: 2 people

INGREDIENTS

- 7 oz Penne pasta
- 2.75 oz Peas
- 2.25 oz Cooked Ham
- 1.7 oz Heavy cream
- 1 tablespoon Extra virgin olive oil
- 1 Small onion
- A pinch of nutmeg
- Black pepper
- Salt
- 1.5 tablespoons Grana Padano cheese

METHOD

1. Finely chop a small onion.
2. Sauté the onion in a pan with a bit of oil over low heat. When the onion is golden brown, add the peas to the pan.
3. Boil a pot of water. Once it boils, salt the water and add the pasta.
4. Cook the peas further, if necessary with some cooking water. Season well with salt and pepper.
5. Dice the ham and add it to the peas in the pan. Mix well to combine all ingredients. Add cream, nutmeg, salt and pepper and mix again.
6. Once the pasta is cooked, drain it and add it to the saucepan, where you sauté it for about a minute to mix everything together.
7. Serve topped with Grana Padano cheese.

Noodles with Fresh Salmon and Red Onions

Difficulty level: very easy
Preparation: 11 min
Cooking time: 16 min
Servings: 2 people

INGREDIENTS

- 6 oz Noodles (any kind)
- 4 oz Salmon without skin
- 4.5 oz Heavy cream
- 2 tablespoons Red onions
- 1 tablespoon Extra virgin olive oil
- Parsley
- Salt

METHOD

1. Cut the salmon into 1 inch pieces.
2. Finely chop the onion.
3. Boil a pot of water. Once it boils, salt the water and add the noodles.
4. Heat a pan with oil and add the onion.
5. Cook the onion for 30 seconds and then add the salmon to the pan.
6. You should cook the salmon for about 3 minutes (or less if you feel it is drying out).
7. Add the cream and cook for another 2 minutes, stirring.
8. When the noodles are cooked, drain them and add them directly to the saucepan.
9. Mix and stir all ingredients over high heat.
10. Serve decorated with parsley.

Smoked Pasta

Difficulty level: easy
Preparation: 16 min
Cooking time: 16 min
Servings: 2 people

INGREDIENTS

- 6.5 oz Noodles (any type)
- 11.5 tablespoons canned tomatoes
- 3.5 oz cream
- 3.25 oz smoked bacon
- 2 tablespoons Parmesan cheese
- 2 tablespoons Emmentaler cheese
- Extra virgin olive oil
- Salt
- Coriander powder
- Nutmeg
- Dried chili pepper
- Black pepper

METHOD

1. Cut the smoked bacon into cubes. Do the same with the Emmentaler cheese.
2. Grate the Parmesan and mix it in a bowl with the Emmentaler cheese.
3. Boil a pot of water. Once it boils, salt the water and add the noodles.
4. Finely chop the nutmeg and chili pepper.
5. Heat a bit of olive oil in a pan and sauté the bacon. Add salt, coriander powder, nutmeg, dried chili pepper, and black pepper to the pan.
6. Stir for 15 seconds, then add the canned tomatoes and cook for about 10 minutes. After 10 minutes, add the cheese mixture and stir until it melts. Add the liquid cream and mix all ingredients together.
7. Once the noodles are cooked, drain them and add them to the sauce pot.
8. Stir thoroughly so that the noodles are combined with the sauce.

Spaghetti with Clams and Beans

Difficulty level: easy
Preparation: 16 min
Cooking time: 16 min
Servings: 2 people

INGREDIENTS

- 6 oz Spaghetti
- 4.5 oz cooked cannellini beans
- 17.75 oz clams
- 1 fresh chili pepper
- 1 garlic clove
- Extra virgin olive oil
- Parsley
- Black pepper
- Salt

METHOD

1. Peel and chop the garlic clove, finely chop the parsley, and slice the chili pepper.
2. Add some oil to a pan, add the garlic, chili pepper, and most of the chopped parsley, and sauté on very low heat.
3. Rinse the clams and clean them by scraping off the outer layer on the surface of the shell. Rinse the clams again and add them to the pan you previously used. Add 1/2 cup of water to the pan and then cover with a lid and cook until the clams open.
4. Once all the clams have opened, turn off the heat, take the fruits out of each clam, and preserve them in a bowl with some of the clam cooking water.
5. Add the clams to the previously used pan. Stir and cook for a few minutes, then add the cannellini beans. Season with salt and pepper and cook for about 7 minutes, until the green beans are very soft.
6. Boil a pot of water. Once it boils, salt the water and add the spaghetti.
7. Once the spaghetti is cooked, drain it and add it to the pan with the sauce, add the parsley from before, and stir quickly.

Pasta with Tuna and Arungula Pesto

Difficulty level: very easy
Preparation: 16 min
Cooking time: 11 min
Servings: 2 people

INGREDIENTS

- 6 oz Pasta (any type)
- Zest of one lemon
- 2.5 oz Tuna fish filets (drained)
- Salt
- 2.25 oz Arugula
- 2 oz small tomatoes
- 2.5 oz extra virgin olive oil
- 2 tablespoons almonds
- Basil
- Salt

METHOD

1. Boil a pot of water. Once it boils, salt the water and add the pasta.
2. Add some basil leaves, almonds, tomatoes, oil, salt, and arugula to a blender. Blend everything until a homogenous cream forms.
3. Add the cream to a pan.
4. Once the pasta is cooked, drain it and add it to the pan with the cream. Add a few tablespoons of pasta cooking water to help the cream warm up.
5. Mix the sauce with the pasta and add the grated lemon zest and drained tuna fish filets. Stir again.

Pasta with Egg and Cheese

Difficulty level: very easy
Preparation: 16 min
Cooking time: 16 min
Servings: 2 people

INGREDIENTS

- 7 oz Pasta (any type)
- 2 tablespoons Parmesan cheese
- 2 tablespoons Pecorino cheese
- 1.5 teaspoon parsley (chopped)
- 3 tablespoons extra virgin olive oil
- 1 garlic clove
- 2 eggs
- Black pepper
- Salt

METHOD

1. Boil a pot of water. Once it boils, salt the water and add the pasta.
2. Beat the eggs in a bowl and add salt and pepper. In the same bowl, add the grated sheep cheese and grated Parmesan. Mix everything together and you get a very flavorful cream.
3. Heat the oil in a pan and sauté the garlic clove for about 30 seconds, then remove it and turn off the heat.
4. In the meantime, the pasta should be done so drain it and add it directly to the pan. Turn off the stove and pour the egg-cheese mixture over the pasta, mixing everything quickly.
5. Serve sprinkled with chopped parsley.

Penne Pasta with Arugula and Chickpea Cream

Difficulty level: easy
Preparation: 11 min
Cooking time: 11 min
Servings: 2 people

INGREDIENTS

- 6 oz Penne Pasta
- 1.75 oz Arugula
- Extra virgin olive oil
- Basil
- 4.5 oz cooked chickpeas
- 2.5 tablespoon Parmesan cheese
- 2 tablespoons leek
- 1.5 tablespoons extra virgin olive oil
- Basil
- Black pepper
- Salt

METHOD

1. Boil a pot of water. Once it boils, salt the water and add the pasta.
2. Heat a bit of oil in a pan. Slice the leek into thin slices and add it to the pan along with the drained chickpeas. Adjust the salt, stir frequently and cook for about 6 minutes.
3. After 6 minutes, turn off the heat and add pepper and basil leaves and stir again.
4. Add the sauce to a blender container, add the grated Parmesan and oil and blend everything with the mixer until a homogenous cream is formed.
5. Let the arugula wilt in a pan with some pasta cooking water for a few minutes and then add the chickpea cream and basil leaves.
6. Once the pasta is cooked, drain it and add it to the pan with the arugula.
7. Stir well to combine all the flavors and serve with some oil and/or ground pepper.

Pasta with Cherry Tomatoes and Anchovies

Difficulty level: very easy
Preparation: 6 min
Cooking time: 11 min
Servings: 2 people

INGREDIENTS

- 7 oz Pasta (any type)
- 2.25 oz cherry tomatoes
- 2 tablespoons extra virgin olive oil
- 1 tablespoon salted anchovies
- 2 basil leaves
- 1 garlic clove
- Fresh chili pepper
- Salt

METHOD

1. Boil a pot of water. Once it boils, salt the water and add the pasta.
2. Wash the cherry tomatoes and cut them into 4 pieces, then halve and quarter them.
3. Take a pot and sauté a garlic clove with some oil for 30 seconds over medium heat. Then remove the clove and add the anchovies. Continue cooking until the anchovies have dissolved, then add the cherry tomatoes and increase the heat until the cherry tomatoes are soft.
4. Now slice the chili pepper thinly and remove the seeds, then add it to the pan with the spices, also add pepper.
5. Once the pasta is cooked, drain it and add it to the sauce pot, stir the sauce and mix it well with the pasta.
6. Serve with basil leaves and a few rolled anchovies.

Spaghetti with Anchovies, Flavored with Orange

Difficulty level: very easy
Preparation: 11 min
Cooking time: 16 min
Servings: 2 people

INGREDIENTS

- 6 oz Spaghetti
- 11 tablespoon Oranges
- 1 garlic clove
- 1.5 tablespoons Cointreau
- 1.5 tablespoons extra virgin olive oil
- 1.5 tablespoons anchovies in oil
- 1 tablespoon breadcrumbs
- 3 mint leaves

METHOD

1. Boil a pot of water. Once it boils, salt the water and add the pasta.
2. Cut the two ends of the orange and peel it, then separate the inner segments with a knife. Cut the segments into small pieces, also cut the anchovy fillets into small pieces.
3. Sauté the garlic clove for 30 seconds in a pan with some oil, then remove it and add the anchovy fillets and orange pieces. Add the Cointreau (this may cause a flame, but don't worry, it will extinguish in a few moments).
4. Use a frying pan to brown the breadcrumbs for a few minutes.
5. Once the spaghetti is cooked, drain it and add it to the pan with the sauce, add the mint leaves and golden breadcrumbs. Stir well to combine all the flavors.

MAIN COURSES

Crispy Salmon

Difficulty level: very easy
Preparation: 11 min
Cooking time: 21 min
Servings: 2 people

INGREDIENTS

- 2 x 9 oz Salmon fillets
- Zest of 1 lemon
- 2 oz breadcrumbs
- 1 sprig parsley
- 1/2 tsp white pepper
- 1 bunch dill
- 2 tablespoons extra virgin olive oil
- 2 sprigs thyme
- 2 sprigs rosemary
- Salt

METHOD

1. Prepare the breadcrumbs by mixing breadcrumbs, dill, thyme, rosemary, parsley, oil, lemon zest, salt, and white pepper in a bowl. Mix until it has a coarse consistency.
2. Take the salmon fillets, remove the skin with a knife and make sure all bones are removed. Place the fillets in a baking dish lined with parchment paper and cover them with the breadcrumbs, pressing them firmly to make them stick to the salmon.
3. Bake in a preheated, ventilated oven at 370°F for 21 minutes. Take the salmon out of the oven and enjoy!

Chicken Breasts in Milk

Difficulty level: easy
Preparation: 16 min
Cooking time: 11 min
Servings: 2 people

INGREDIENTS

- 1.5 tablespoons Butter
- Black pepper
- 3 oz Whole milk
- 1.5 teaspoon Extra virgin olive oil
- Wheat flour
- 11.5 tablespoons Chicken breast (sliced)
- 2 sprigs Thyme
- Salt

METHOD

1. Take the chicken breast slices and use a meat pounder to make thinner slices.
2. Take a pan, add a little oil and a piece of butter and heat it on low flame until the butter melts.
3. Meanwhile, coat the chicken slices in flour and place them in the pan. Now turn the heat to medium to high and fry the slices for 3-4 minutes until they form a crust. Add salt and pepper and cover the pan for an additional 3 minutes so the milk thickens. Serve and enjoy hot!

Mushroom Escalopes

Difficulty level: easy
Preparation: 21 min
Cooking time: 11 min
Servings: 2 people

INGREDIENTS

- 1 Garlic Clove
- 7 oz Veal
- 2 tablespoons Butter
- Black Pepper
- 9 oz Mushrooms
- 1 Sprig of Chopped Rosemary
- 1.5 tablespoons Wheat Flour
- 1.5 teaspoon Extra Virgin Olive Oil
- Salt
- Thyme

METHOD

1. Use a meat pounder to make the veal slices thinner. Now take the flour and flour the slices well on both sides. Remove the excess flour and set it aside.
2. Wash the mushrooms well and slice them thinly, then set them aside.
3. Take a frying pan, melt half of the butter (about 2.5 teaspoons) and add some oil. Add the floured veal slices, salt and pepper, and fry for 3 minutes on each side. When the meat is golden brown, transfer it to a plate.
4. In the same pan you fried the meat in, add a garlic clove, chopped rosemary, and half of the remaining butter. Melt the butter and then fry the mushrooms. Season with salt and pepper.
5. Add the reserved veal slices back to the pan with the mushrooms, add the thyme and a ladle of water, and let the flavors mix well for 1-2 minutes on low heat.
6. Now serve the slices and enjoy them hot!

Chicken with Soy Sauce

Difficulty level: easy
Preparation: 21 min
Cooking time: 11 min
Servings: 2 people
Hinweis: Marinierzeit des Huhns 2 Stunden

INGREDIENTS

- 1.5 teaspoon Cayenne Pepper
- 9 oz Chicken Breast
- 0.2 tablespoons Fresh Ginger
- 2 oz Soy Sauce
- 1 tablespoon Wildflower Honey
- Zest of 1 Lime
- Juice of Half a Lime
- Garlic Clove
- Extra Virgin Olive Oil

METHOD

1. Cut the chicken into bite-sized pieces and place them in a bowl. Pour the soy sauce over it and let the chicken marinate.
2. Melt the honey in a pot for a few minutes, let it cool and then add it to the bowl with the chicken.
3. Add the cayenne pepper, lime juice and crushed garlic to the bowl.
4. Grate the ginger and add it to the bowl.
5. Mix all the ingredients well together and seal the bowl with plastic wrap.
6. Place the bowl in the refrigerator for at least 2 hours to marinate.
7. Take a pan and heat some oil, add the marinated chicken along with the liquid from the bowl.
8. Cook for 11 minutes on high heat, turning the chicken pieces frequently, or until the marinade is dry and the honey is caramelized.
9. Salt may not be necessary, but add it if you feel it's needed.
10. Serve the chicken in soy sauce hot and enjoy!

Lemon Escalopes

Difficulty level: easy
Preparation: 11 min
Cooking time: 11 min
Servings: 2 people

INGREDIENTS

- Schwarzer Pfeffer
- 4 Scheiben vom Kalbfleisch
- Weizenmehl
- 1 tbsp Zitronensaft
- Salz
- 1 tbsp Butter

METHOD

1. Squeeze the lemon and pour the juice into a bowl.
2. Use a meat pounder to pound the veal slices to make them softer. Dip the slices in the flour and coat them well on both sides. Remove any excess flour.
3. Heat the butter in a frying pan. Once it's melted, add the slices and fry them for a few minutes on each side until they are well browned.
4. Add salt and pepper. Now add the lemon juice and cook for an additional 3 minutes.
5. When the lemon starts to thicken, transfer the slices to a plate and serve hot!

Sole with Milk

Difficulty level: very easy
Preparation: 16 min
Cooking time: 11 min
Servings: 2 people

INGREDIENTS

- Salt
- 2.25 oz Butter
- 2 medium sized Sole
- Wheat flour
- Juice of one lemon
- 1 sprig of parsley
- Whole milk

METHOD

1. Clean and wash the Seezungen and then dry them well. Soak the Seezungen in milk and then flour them well on both sides.
2. Take a frying pan and add butter and a drop of water. Once they are melted, add the Seezunge and cook for 4 minutes or until they are golden brown.
3. In the meantime, squeeze one lemon and add the juice to a separate bowl. Chop some parsley with a knife.
4. Once the Seezunge is finished, place it on a plate, pour the lemon juice over it, and add a little parsley and a pinch of salt!

Meat in Sauce

Difficulty level: very easy
Preparation: 6 min
Cooking time: 16 min
Servings: 2 people

INGREDIENTS

- Extra virgin olive oil
- 5.25 oz beef slices
- Oregano
- Salt
- 3.5 oz canned tomatoes
- Black pepper
- 1 garlic clove

METHOD

1. Take a pan, add some oil and fry a garlic clove.
2. Now add the canned tomatoes with a little water, salt and pepper. Let it cook for 11 minutes and then add the beef slices. Cover the slices well with the sauce and add the oregano.
3. Cover the pan with a lid and cook for an additional 4 minutes, turning the slices frequently.
4. Serve and enjoy hot!

Chicken Strips

Difficulty level: very easy
Preparation: 11 min
Cooking time: 11 min
Servings: 2 people

INGREDIENTS

- All-purpose flour
- 12.5 oz chicken breast
- 1 garlic clove
- Salt
- 2 tablespoons extra virgin olive oil
- Black pepper
- Parsley

METHOD

1. Take the chicken and cut it into pieces, then dip it in the flour and remove the excess with a sieve.
2. Heat a pan with some oil and add a garlic clove over low to medium flame.
3. Season with salt and pepper and cook for 4 minutes on high heat, stirring often so the meat does not burn.
4. Then add the chopped parsley.
5. Enjoy the chicken strips hot!

Baked Cod Fillets

Difficulty level: easy
Preparation: 11 min
Cooking time: 16 min
Servings: 2 people

INGREDIENTS

- 1.5 tablespoons extra virgin olive oil
- 2 tablespoons breadcrumbs
- Juice and zest of 1 lemon
- 7 oz cod fillet
- 1.5 teaspoon slivered almonds
- 3 sprigs thyme
- Black pepper
- Salt

METHOD

1. Take a bowl and add the breadcrumbs, thyme, lemon zest and lemon juice. Add the slivered almonds, salt and pepper. Mix all the ingredients together to combine.
2. Take the cod fillets and ensure that all bones are removed.
3. Place the fillets in a bowl, drizzle with some olive oil and add the breadcrumbs mixture you previously made. Spread the breadcrumbs mixture with your hands on the fillets.
4. Take a baking dish, add a little oil and put the fish in.
5. If you have some breadcrumbs mixture left, add it to the fillets.
6. Bake the fish in preheated oven at 390°F for 20 minutes or until crispy.
7. Put on a plate and enjoy!

Swordfish with Olives

Difficulty level: very easy
Preparation: 16 min
Cooking time: 11 min
Servings: 2 people

INGREDIENTS

- 10 oz tomatoes
- 1.5 oz pitted green olives
- Salt
- 2 tablespoons extra virgin olive oil
- 1 garlic clove
- 1.5 teaspoon pine nuts
- 10 oz swordfish sliced
- Oregano
- Black pepper

METHOD

1. Take the cherry tomatoes and cut them in half.
2. Add a little oil in a pan and fry a garlic clove. Once the garlic turns golden, add the cherry tomatoes and cook for 11 minutes. Add salt and oregano.
3. Meanwhile, cut the pitted olives into rings and add them to the pan.
4. Now remove the garlic clove and add the swordfish slices, cook for about 3 minutes per side. Pepper and cover with a lid.
5. While the swordfish cooks, roast the pine nuts in a small pan, being careful not to burn them.
6. When the fish is cooked, transfer it to a plate and add the roasted pine nuts.
7. Enjoy it hot!

Eggplant Cordon Bleu

Difficulty level: very easy
Preparation: 11 min
Cooking time: 17 min
Servings: 2 Stück

INGREDIENTS

- 2.25 oz smoked provola cheese
- 4 oz eggplant
- 2 basil leaves
- 2.12 tablespoons cooked ham, sliced
- 2 eggs
- Salt
- Breadcrumbs
- All-purpose flour
- Black pepper
- Peanut oil

METHOD

1. Wash the eggplant, remove the ends and cut it into 0.5 inch thick slices.
2. Place the slices in a colander and salt them. Let them sit for about 30 minutes. This process serves to remove the water naturally present in the eggplant.
3. Take the smoked provola cheese and cut it into thin slices.
4. Prepare the breadcrumbs. Beat the two eggs in a bowl, add salt and pepper.
5. Take two bowls, one with the flour and the other with the breadcrumbs.
6. After 30 minutes, take the eggplant out of the colander, wash it well and dry it off.
7. Place the eggplant slices on a plate, fill it with cooked ham, basil and provola cheese. Place another eggplant slice on top, as if it were a sandwich.
8. Now we move on to the breadcrumbs. Take the eggplant sandwich (with ham and provola), flour it on both sides, dip it in the eggs and then in the breadcrumbs. Spread the breadcrumbs evenly.
9. Take a frying pan, add the oil and heat it. Dip the cordon bleus in it and fry them for about two minutes until golden brown. Let them drain and place them on paper towels.
10. You can also bake them in the oven. Preheat the oven to 390°F and bake the cordon bleus for 20 minutes, turning them after 10 minutes.
11. And now enjoy it hot!

Sautéed Beef with Arugula and Cherry Tomatoes

Difficulty level: easy
Preparation: 11 min
Cooking time: 11 min
Servings: 2 people
Hinweis: Nimm das Fleisch 1 Stunde vorher aus dem Kühlschrank.

INGREDIENTS

- 2 oz arugula
- 2 oz cherry tomatoes
- 14.5 oz sirloin steak
- Extra virgin olive oil
- Sea salt flakes
- Black pepper

METHOD

1. Take the meat out of the refrigerator 1 hour before cooking.
2. Wash the arugula and dry it. Wash the cherry tomatoes and cut them in half.
3. Take the meat, which now has room temperature, and remove the fat parts. Cut it into 1 inch thick slices.
4. Place the grill on the fire and heat it over a high flame.
5. Now, that it's hot, reduce the heat, place the meat on it and grill for 4 minutes per side. (help yourself with tongs, so the juice stays in the meat.)
6. If you use a food thermometer, you should know that the optimal temperature in the middle of the meat should be around 125°.
7. Take a wooden cutting board, place a bed of arugula on it and then place the meat on it.
8. Cut the meat into diagonal stripes, add cherry tomatoes

Beef Strips

Difficulty level: easy
Preparation: 16 min
Cooking time: 16 min
Servings: 2 people

INGREDIENTS

- 2 tablespoons vegetable broth or hot water
- 1.5 tablespoons Parmesan cheese
- 1 tablespoon balsamic vinegar
- 11.5 tablespoons sirloin or rump steak
- 1 tablespoon all-purpose flour
- 1 tablespoon extra virgin olive oil
- Black pepper
- 1.75 oz arugula
- Salt

METHOD

1. Wash the arugula and place it in a bowl. Season with salt, pepper, extra virgin olive oil and balsamic vinegar. Set aside.
2. Heat the vegetable broth or hot water.
3. Now, prepare the Parmesan waffles. Preheat the oven to 350°F. Take a baking tray and place a sheet of parchment paper on it. Pile the Parmesan cheese on top and form it with a spoon as desired (round, elongated, square). Place the tray in the oven and bake for 10 minutes or until golden brown.
4. Meanwhile, take the meat and cut it into strips. Place the meat in a sieve and add the flour. Make sure the whole meat is well floured, then remove the excess flour.
5. Take a pan, add some olive oil and the meat strips. Cook them for a few minutes until a crust forms. Season with pepper and salt. Add two or three tablespoons of vegetable broth or water. Cook until you get a creamy consistency. Then the meat is ready.
6. Serve the meat with a bowl of arugula and enjoy!

Salmon Fillets with Black Olives and Cherry Tomatoes

Difficulty level: very easy
Preparation: 11 min
Cooking time: 16 min
Servings: 2 people
Note: 1 hour marination of cherry tomatoes

INGREDIENTS

- 14 oz Norwegian salmon
- 6 oz cherry tomatoes
- 1 sprig dried oregano
- 1 tablespoon extra virgin olive oil
- Salt
- 1 garlic clove
- 2.5 tablespoon pitted black olives
- 0.2 tablespoons pickled capers

METHOD

1. Wash the cherry tomatoes and cut them into 4 pieces.
2. Place them in a bowl, add the halved garlic, oregano, oil, and salt.
3. Mix the ingredients well and cover the bowl with plastic wrap.
4. Allow the cherry tomatoes to marinate for 1 hour.
5. After an hour, begin cooking the salmon.
6. Remove the skin from the salmon and make sure to remove all bones.
7. Cut it into 2 fillets.
8. Take the bowl with the cherry tomatoes and remove the garlic.
9. Take a baking dish, add some extra virgin olive oil and add the cherry tomatoes with the dressing.
10. Place the salmon fillets on top of the cherry tomatoes and add a few cherry tomatoes on top of the salmon to give it flavor.
11. Add salt, pepper, black olives and capers.
12. Preheat the oven to 350°F and bake the dish for 15 minutes.
13. Now everything is ready to enjoy the salmon fillets with black olives and cherry tomatoes!

Swordfish Rolls

Difficulty level: very easy
Preparation: 16 min
Cooking time: 11 min
Servings: 2 people

INGREDIENTS

- 2 swordfish fillets
- 4 basil leaves
- 1.75 oz tomatoes
- 2 teaspoon capers in salt
- Salt
- Chili powder
- 1 garlic clove
- 1 tablespoon green olives
- 1 tablespoon extra virgin olive oil
- 2 basil leaves
- 1.5 tablespoons breadcrumbs
- 2.5 oz Auburn tomatoes

METHOD

1. Chop the olives and capers with a knife and cut the tomatoes into small cubes.
2. Finely chop the garlic.
3. Take a bowl for the filling, add the breadcrumbs, capers, olives, a teaspoon of chili, fresh basil, salt, and a splash of extra virgin olive oil.
4. Set aside.
5. Take the swordfish, halve the two fillets and fill them with the filling you previously made. Press the edges well so that the filling does not leak out, and roll them into a roulade.
6. Secure the roll with toothpicks.
7. Take a tomato, slice it and set it aside.
8. Take a baking dish, pour a little oil in it, place the rolls in it, stick a basil leaf on one side of the roll and a tomato slice on the other side.
9. Season with olive oil and sprinkle with breadcrumbs.
10. Preheat the oven to 350°F, place the baking dish in the oven and bake for 11 minutes.
11. And now enjoy it hot!

Stuffed Chicken Rolls

Difficulty level: easy
Preparation: 16 min
Cooking time: 11 min
Servings: 2 people

INGREDIENTS

- Black pepper
- Salt
- 2 tablespoons oil
- 7 oz chicken breast
- 4 sprigs rosemary
- 4 slices Scamorza (Provola) cheese
- 4 slices bacon

METHOD

1. Take the 4 chicken slices and crush them with a meat mallet. Now that you have the thin slices, place the bacon and cheese on each slice. Roll up the ingredients and secure the roll with a skewer. Season the rolls with rosemary, pepper, and salt.
2. Take the grill, grease it with a little oil and heat it up well. Once hot, grill the skewers and turn them occasionally. (You can also cook them in a pan).
3. Serve the rolls and enjoy them hot!

Pork with Marsala Wine

Difficulty level: easy
Preparation: 16 min
Cooking time: 11 min
Servings: 2 people

INGREDIENTS

- 1.75 oz Marsala wine
- 4 slices of pork loin
- 1.5 tablespoons extra virgin olive oil
- 2.5 tablespoon vegetable broth
- Salt
- 2 tablespoons butter
- Wheat flour
- Black pepper

METHOD

1. Take the slices and pound them with a meat mallet. Flour the slices and remove excess flour.
2. Take a frying pan, add some oil and add a piece of butter. When the butter has melted, add the pork slices and fry them on medium heat for 2 minutes per side. Season the meat with Marsala, add pepper and salt.
3. Now add the vegetable broth (or hot water) and cook for a few more minutes until a sauce forms.
4. Now serve and enjoy!

Chicken Breast with Cornflakes

Difficulty level: easy
Preparation: 16 min
Cooking time: 6 min
Servings: 2 people

INGREDIENTS

- 1.75 oz cornflakes
- 1.5 teaspoon whole milk
- 1.5 teaspoon spicy paprika
- 1 egg
- 11 tablespoon chicken breast
- Salt
- 1 bunch chives
- 2 teaspoon extra virgin olive oil
- 1 garlic clove
- 1.75 oz cucumber
- 1.5 teaspoon white wine vinegar
- 3.5 oz Greek yogurt
- Salt
- Peanut oil

METHOD

1. Take a bowl, add the yogurt and a very finely chopped garlic clove. Then add oil, chopped chives, white wine and a pinch of salt. Mix all ingredients very well together.
2. Take the cucumber, wash it, cut off the ends and grate it directly into the bowl. Mix well.
3. Take the bowl, cover it with plastic wrap and put it in the refrigerator.
4. Take the cornflakes, put them in a clear bag and crush them with a rolling pin.
5. Place the crushed cornflakes in a baking dish and add the paprika powder and mix well.
6. Take another baking dish and add the beaten egg, milk and salt. Mix well.
7. Take the chicken breasts, sprinkle them with paprika, place them in the egg and turn them over.
8. Then dip them in the bowl with the cornflake crumbs and let them stick well on both sides of the chicken. Place them aside.
9. Take a frying pan, add some peanut oil and fry the chicken breasts for 5 minutes per side. (You can also bake them for 15 minutes at 350°F in the oven).
10. Place the chicken breasts on a tray with paper towels.
11. Serve the dish hot with the yogurt sauce!

Pork Tenderloin

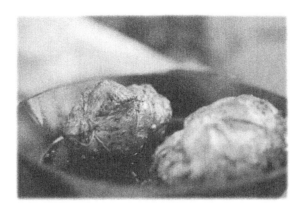

Difficulty level: very easy
Preparation: 21 min
Cooking time: 11 min
Servings: 2 people

INGREDIENTS

- 8 oz pork tenderloin
- 2 tablespoons butter
- 6 green peppercorns
- 4 slices smoked bacon
- 8 sage leaves
- 4 sprigs rosemary
- Salt
- 1.5 teaspoon extra virgin olive oil
- 1 tablespoon butter
- Salt
- Extra virgin olive oil
- 4 onions

METHOD

1. Take the pork slices and wrap them with bacon.
2. Cover the slices with two sage leaves and use your hands to stick them to the bacon.
3. Tie them together with twine and make a double knot to secure them. Cut off the excess twine.
4. Take the spring onions and cut them into quarters. Take a non-stick pan, add butter, oil and the spring onions. Fry them well. Turn off the flame, but keep them warm.
5. Add the butter, oil and rosemary to another pan. Place the tenderloins on top and brown them on both sides. Add green peppercorns.
6. Now serve the pork tenderloins with spring onions and enjoy!

Pan-seared Cod Filet

Difficulty level: easy
Preparation: 1q min
Cooking time: 11 min
Servings: 2 people

INGREDIENTS

- 2 x 7 oz cod filets
- 1 tablespoon pine nuts
- 1.5 oz butter
- 2 tablespoons all-purpose flour
- Salt
- Black pepper
- 1.5 teaspoon parsley, chopped
- 2.5 oz water

METHOD

1. Toast the pine nuts in a pan for 3 minutes and stir well. Then set them aside.
2. Now finely chop the parsley and set it aside.
3. Add the butter to a frying pan and melt it on a low flame.
4. Meanwhile, add the flour to a baking dish and add salt and pepper.
5. Once the butter is melted, coat the cod filets in the flour mixture and place them in the pan.
6. Cook the cod filets for 3 minutes on each side. Then place them on a plate and set them aside.
7. In the same pan that you cooked the cod in, add some water and turn the heat up for a few minutes. A creamy sauce will form and you need to add the chopped parsley, salt and pepper. Stir well for 5 minutes.
8. Now plate the cod filets, pour the freshly prepared sauce over them and add the toasted pine nuts.
9. Serve and enjoy!

Bolognese Cutlet

Difficulty level: easy
Preparation: 16 min
Cooking time: 11 Minuten
Servings: 2 people

INGREDIENTS

- 2 slices of veal
- 1/2 cup bread crumbs
- 1/4 cup all-purpose flour
- 1 medium egg
- 1 tablespoon butter
- 5.5 oz raw ham
- 3 oz Parmesan cheese
- 1/2 cup beef broth

METHOD

1. Heat the beef or vegetable broth.
2. Pound the meat with a meat mallet and set aside.
3. Prepare 3 bowls. Add the flour to the first. In the second, beat the eggs. Add the bread crumbs to the third.
4. Take the meat and dip it in the flour, coating both sides well.
5. Dip the floured slices in the eggs and then in the bowl with the bread crumbs.
6. Press the bread crumbs well into the slices so they stick together.
7. Take a pan, add a little oil and some butter and fry the slices. Turn them several times so they become golden brown. Now immediately add the ham and grate the Parmesan cheese on top. Add a ladle of broth and continue cooking for 6 minutes. Let all the water evaporate and place the slices on a serving platter.
8. And now enjoy them hot!

Kale-Burger

Difficulty level: easy
Preparation: 11 min
Cooking time: 17 min
Servings: 2 Stück

INGREDIENTS

- 4 oz black kale
- Salt
- 3.5 oz sandwich bread
- Extra virgin olive oil
- 1.5 oz water
- 1 egg
- 2 oz Grana Padano cheese
- Parsley
- Black pepper

METHOD

1. Wash the black kale and coarsely chop it with a knife.
2. Take a pan, add some oil, and add the black kale. Cook for 11 minutes, until it has wilted.
3. Take a bowl and add the diced bread. Pour in the water and knead it with your hands until the dough is smooth.
4. Finely chop the parsley and set it aside. Grate the Grana Padano cheese and set it aside.
5. Now add the hot black kale, Grana Padano cheese, egg, chopped parsley, salt, and pepper to the bowl with the bread dough. Mix the ingredients with your hands until a homogeneous mixture is formed.
6. Take a dough cutter, add the dough, press it down with your fingers, remove the cutter, and you have the classic burger shape.
7. Take a frying pan, add some oil, and fry the burgers for 5 minutes, turning them often so they do not burn.
8. Now serve them and enjoy!

Fried Calamari

Difficulty level: easy
Preparation: 21 min
Cooking time: 11 min
Servings: 2 people

INGREDIENTS

- 14 oz Calamari
- 3.5 oz all-purpose flour
- Salt
- Peanut oil

METHOD

1. Wash the calamari under running water and separate the head from the body of the squid.
2. Remove the cartilage and the innards carefully from the body. Take a knife now and slice it open to remove the skin and fins.
3. Slice the body into less than 0.5 inch thick rings. Slice the tentacles off and place them in a colander to remove the water.
4. Place the flour in a bowl and coat the calamari well. Use a sieve to remove any excess flour.
5. Pour some oil in a pan and heat it. Once hot, add the calamari and fry for 4 minutes, turning them often so they brown evenly.
6. Once they are crispy, remove them and place them on a tray lined with paper towels to remove excess oil.
7. Now season with salt to taste and enjoy the fried calamari while it's hot!

Chicken nuggets with Yogurt

Difficulty level: very easy
Preparation: 11 min
Cooking time: 16 min
Servings: 2 people

INGREDIENTS

- Extra virgin olive oil
- 2 tablespoons Pinenuts
- 9 oz Chicken breast
- 1.5 teaspoon All-purpose flour
- 2.25 oz Water
- Salt
- 1 teaspoon Turmeric powder
- 3.5 oz Nonfat yogurt

METHOD

1. Remove the fat from the chicken and cut it into about 0.8 inch cubes.
2. Place the chicken in a bowl, add the flour and salt and mix well, making sure the meat is covered. Remove any excess flour with a sieve.
3. Take a frying pan, add some oil and roast the pinenuts for 3 minutes on high heat.
4. Now add the chicken and cook for 2 minutes. Then add the water.
5. Meanwhile, take a bowl and add the yogurt and turmeric. Stir until the mixture is smooth.
6. Pour the resulting sauce into the pan and mix all the ingredients well.
7. Serve the treats now and enjoy them while they are still hot!

Pork tenderloin with Honey and Ginger

Difficulty level: easy
Preparation: 16 min
Cooking time: 11 min
Servings: 2 people

INGREDIENTS

- 9 oz Pork tenderloin
- 1 tablespoon fresh ginger
- 1 tsp soy sauce
- 1 tbsp wildflower honey
- 1 tbsp sesame oil
- 0.2 tablespoons fresh chili pepper
- Salt

METHOD

1. Take the meat and remove any excess fat, then cut it into 0.75 inch cubes.
2. Lightly salt the meat.
3. Take the chili pepper, remove the seeds and cut them into thin strips.
4. Take the ginger, peel it and cut it into thin slices.
5. Add some oil to a frying pan and heat it up. Add the ginger and after two minutes add the chili pepper.
6. Let the oil infuse for a few minutes, turn the heat to medium and add the pork tenderloin cubes to the pan.
7. Fry the cubes for 4 minutes until they are slightly crispy. Now add the honey and soy sauce and cook for another 5 minutes.
8. Once the sauce has thickened, serve the tenderloin and enjoy!

Eggs and Peas

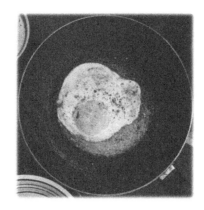

Difficulty level: very easy
Preparation: 6 min
Cooking time: 16 min
Servings: 2 people

INGREDIENTS

- 2 eggs
- Extra virgin olive oil
- Black pepper
- 14 oz peas
- 2 tablespoons onions
- Salt

METHOD

1. Take an onion and chop it finely.
2. Add some oil to a pan and sauté the onions on medium heat.
3. Now add the peas, salt, and pepper and add a cup of water. Cook for another 11 minutes and stir occasionally.
4. Once the water has evaporated, add in the two eggs and be careful not to break the yolks. Put a lid on the pan.
5. Cook to your desired consistency. Season with salt and pepper and enjoy!

Salmon steak with Tomatoes and Thyme

Difficulty level: easy
Preparation: 11 min
Cooking time: 11 min
Servings: 2 people

INGREDIENTS

- 11 tablespoon Auburn tomatoes
- 1 garlic clove
- 3 branches of thyme
- Extra virgin olive oil
- 11 tablespoon salmon fillet
- Salt
- Black pepper

METHOD

1. Take the salmon steak, remove the skin and bones. Cut 2 slices, season with salt and pepper and set aside. Wash and dice the tomatoes. Place them in boiling water for 30 seconds. Chop the thyme.
2. Place the salmon slices in an oiled non-stick pan, add a crushed garlic clove and fry on high flame for 2 minutes on each side.
3. Now add the tomatoes and thyme and cook for an additional 6 minutes.

Cutlet with Ham and Cheese

Difficulty level: very easy
Preparation: 16 min
Cooking time: 6 min
Servings: 4 people

INGREDIENTS

- 1 sprig of rosemary
- 4 slices of pork loin
- 4 slices of provolone cheese
- Black pepper
- Salt
- 1.5 tablespoons butter
- 1.75 oz diced cooked ham
- 2 tablespoons wheat flour
- 2 leaves of sage

METHOD

1. Pound the pork slices with a meat mallet to make them thinner.
2. Place flour, salt, and pepper in a bowl. Place the meat on top and coat well on both sides.
3. Take a pan, add a little oil and a piece of butter, and let it melt.
4. When the butter is fully melted, add 2 sage leaves and some rosemary. Fry for a few seconds and then remove the herbs with tongs.
5. Place the meat in the same pan and fry for a few seconds to form a crust.
6. Chop the remaining sage leaves and rosemary. Cut the provolone cheese into slices.
7. Now place the meat on a plate, add the provolone cheese, diced ham, and chopped herbs.
8. Serve and enjoy the schnitzel!

Chicken Breasts with Mustard and Herbs

Difficulty level: easy
Preparation: 16 min
Cooking time: 16 min
Servings: 2 people
Note: 30 minutes marinating time

INGREDIENTS

- Bread crumbs
- 2 leaves of sage
- 1 sprig of rosemary
- 1 sprig of parsley
- White pepper
- 1 tablespoon butter
- 3 tablespoons mustard
- 11 tablespoon chicken breast, sliced
- Extra virgin olive oil
- 1 lemon juice
- 1 pinch of salt

METHOD

1. Take a bowl, squeeze the lemon and pour the juice, add 2 tablespoons of olive oil and a pinch of salt.
2. Chop the herbs and add half of them to the bowl. Set the other half aside. Stir well.
3. Take a container, place the chicken slices on it and pour the marinade sauce over it. Allow it to rest for 30 minutes.
4. Take a pan, pour some of the marinade sauce and add the drained chicken. Cook until the chicken is golden brown. Add salt.
5. Drain the chicken breasts, place them in a container and sprinkle with mustard. Then dip them in bread crumbs.
6. Heat some butter and a little oil in a pan and fry the chicken slices for a few minutes.
7. Add the herbs and pepper set aside.
8. Place the crispy chicken breasts on a plate and enjoy!

Turkey Cutlets

Difficulty level: easy
Preparation: 21 min
Cooking time: 11 min
Servings: 2 people

INGREDIENTS

- 1 egg
- Extra virgin olive oil
- 2 large turkey cutlets
- Salt
- Black pepper
- 1 small fresh chili pepper
- 1.5 teaspoon capers in salt
- 3.5 oz bread crumbs
- Parsley
- 1.75 oz extra virgin olive oil
- 1 tablespoon pitted black olives
- 1 garlic clove
- 6.25 oz cherry tomatoes
- 1 garlic clove
- 1 teaspoon oregano
- Extra virgin olive oil
- Salt
- Black pepper

METHOD

1. Wash and cut the cherry tomatoes. Chop a garlic clove, add salt, pepper and oregano. Put everything in a bowl, dress with oil, cover with film and put in the refrigerator.
2. Now cut the chili pepper, remove the seeds and chop it finely.
3. Wash the capers and olives and chop them with a knife. Place in a bowl and set aside.
4. Chop the parsley.
5. Take a pan and add the olive oil, a garlic clove, chopped chili pepper, olives and capers. Stir for a minute and then add the breadcrumbs. Roast well over high heat. Don't forget to remove the garlic.
6. Now put the contents of the pan in a casserole dish, add the parsley and let it cool.
7. Take a large bowl, beat the egg, add salt and pepper and quickly beat the ingredients together.
8. Dip the turkey slices in the egg and then in the bread crumbs and press them firmly so that the breadcrumbs stick to the meat.
9. Fry the cutlets in a pan until crispy.
10. Let them drain well in paper towels to remove excess oil.
11. Now serve and enjoy!

Beef Carpaccio with Arugola and Parmesan

Difficulty level: easy
Preparation: 16 min
Servings: 2 people

INGREDIENTS

- 1.75 oz arugula
- 7 oz beef tenderloin
- 1.75 oz grated Grana Padano cheese
- 2.5 tablespoon lemon juice
- Black pepper
- 1.75 oz extra virgin olive oil
- Salt

METHOD

1. Squeeze the lemon in a bowl to extract the juice, then add pepper, salt, and oil. Mix well with a whisk.
2. Place the arugula on a plate and top with very thinly sliced meat slices, using a deli slicer.
3. Add the cheese flakes, pour the previously prepared sauce on top, and garnish with lemon slices.
4. The dish is now ready to enjoy!

Scrambled Eggs

Difficulty level: very easy
Preparation: 6 min
Cooking time: 6 min
Servings: 2 people

INGREDIENTS

- 4 medium eggs
- Extra virgin olive oil
- Salt
- Black pepper

METHOD

1. Whisk 4 eggs in a bowl, add salt and pepper, and mix well to combine.
2. Now heat some oil in a frying pan and pour the contents of the bowl in. As it starts to cook, break the mixture with a spoon and continue to cook.
3. Serve your scrambled eggs now with a piece of toasted bread!

Salmon Burgers

Difficulty level: easy
Preparation: 16 min
Cooking time: 4 min
Servings: 2 people

INGREDIENTS

- 7 oz salmon fillet
- 2 tablespoons breadcrumbs
- 1 fresh spring onion
- 1 tablespoon chopped dill
- 1 tablespoon mild mustard
- Extra virgin olive oil
- 1 fresh chili
- 1 egg
- Salt
- Black pepper

METHOD

1. Remove the skin and bones from the salmon and then cut it into cubes.
2. Chop the spring onion, dill and half the chili pepper, removing the inner seeds.
3. Place the salmon cubes in a bowl, add the spring onion, chili, and dill and mix well. Season with salt and pepper.
4. Add the egg and breadcrumbs to the bowl and gently mix to combine.
5. Form the mixture into 2 burgers.
6. Heat a skillet with some oil and cook the burgers for 3 minutes per side.
7. Now that the burgers are done, you can serve them with sauces of your choice or as a sandwich!

Peppers with Eggs

Difficulty level: easy
Preparation: 16 min
Cooking time: 11 min
Servings: 2 people

INGREDIENTS

- 2 tablespoons extra virgin olive oil
- 4 eggs
- 1/2 green pepper
- 1/2 red pepper
- 1/2 yellow pepper
- Salt
- Black pepper

METHOD

1. Take peppers that have a very wavy shape so that when cut, they look like flowers.
2. Place the red, yellow, and green peppers on the cutting board and slice them into about 0.75 inch thick slices, being careful that the pepper ring does not break.
3. Take a non-stick skillet and add some oil to it. Once hot, add the pepper rings and let them fry for a few seconds on both sides.
4. Crack an egg into a bowl, but be careful not to break the yolk. Carefully pour the egg into the pepper that's in the skillet.
5. Now cover with a lid and cook.
6. To serve, remove the egg whites that have come loose from the pepper shape, season with salt and pepper, and enjoy!

Scampi with Tomatoes and Breadcrumbs

Difficulty level: easy
Preparation: 11 min
Cooking time: 21 min
Servings: 2 people

INGREDIENTS

- 1 tablespoon of chopped parsley
- 1.25 lbs of scampi
- Extra virgin olive oil
- 5.5 oz of peeled tomatoes
- Salt
- 1 tablespoon of breadcrumbs
- 1 clove of garlic
- 1 fresh chili pepper

METHOD

1. Wash the scampi and cut off the skin on the back and belly using scissors.
2. Take a pan, add some oil and fry a clove of garlic. Add a chili pepper as well.
3. When the garlic is golden brown, add the breadcrumbs and mix quickly. Add the scampi quickly.
4. Then add the peeled and diced tomatoes, and put a lid on the pan.
5. Cook for 15 minutes.
6. In the meantime, chop the parsley.
7. After 15 minutes, remove the garlic and chili from the pan. Serve the scampi and sprinkle with chopped parsley.
8. Enjoy now!

Turkey Rolls

Difficulty level: very easy
Preparation: 16 min
Cooking time: 8 min
Servings: 2 people

INGREDIENTS

- 8 oz turkey breast
- Black pepper
- 2.5 oz cooked ham
- 2 eggs
- 2.75 oz Emmentaler cheese
- Bread crumbs
- Salt
- Peanut oil

METHOD

1. Pound the meat with a meat mallet to make the chicken slices thinner.
2. In a bowl, whisk two eggs, add salt and pepper, and mix well.
3. Dip the turkey slices in the egg mixture and then coat both sides in breadcrumbs.
4. Place a slice of cheese and a piece of cooked ham on each slice.
5. Roll up the slices one by one and secure them with toothpicks.
6. Fry them in a pan with oil and turn them often to cook evenly. Place them on paper towels to remove excess oil.
7. Serve the rolls and enjoy them hot!

Plaice Fillets in Sauce

Difficulty level: easy
Preparation: 11 min
Cooking time: 16 min
Servings: 2 people

INGREDIENTS

- 4.5 oz Plaice (2 fillets)
- 7 oz strained tomatoes
- 1 tablespoon extra virgin olive oil
- 1 tablespoon pitted black olives
- 1 tablespoon wheat flour
- 3 basil leaves
- 2 sprigs oregano
- 1 clove of garlic
- Black pepper
- Salt

METHOD

1. Cut the black olives into thin slices and add them to a pan with oil and a clove of garlic. Add the canned tomatoes, salt, and pepper. Cook on low heat for about 10 minutes, stirring occasionally.
2. Finely chop the oregano and mix it with flour, salt, and pepper.
3. Dip the sole fillets in the flour mixture, making sure both sides are well coated.
4. Heat a small amount of oil in a pan and cook the fillets for a few minutes on each side.
5. Then add the fillets to the pan with the sauce and cook for an additional 2 minutes. Serve garnished with basil leaves.

Pork Chops with Lemon

Difficulty level: very easy
Preparation: 16 min
Cooking time: 11 min
Servings: 2 people

INGREDIENTS

- 2 Pork chops
- 2 sprigs of thyme
- Zest of half a lemon
- Salt
- 1 tablespoon of extra virgin olive oil
- 1/4 cup of red beer
- 1 tablespoon of butter
- 1/2 clove of garlic
- 1 sprig of rosemary

METHOD

1. Finely chop the herbs and garlic, and zest the lemon.
2. Place the pork chops on a cutting board and season them with salt and pepper. Heat a pan with some oil and add the pork chops, cook for 6 minutes on each side. Remove the pork chops from the pan and set them aside.
3. In the same pan, add the chopped herbs, butter, and garlic. Let it thicken.
4. Place the pork chops on a plate and pour the sauce over them. Serve hot and enjoy!

Plaice Fillets with Herbs

Difficulty level: very easy
Preparation: 11 min
Cooking time: 21 min
Servings: 2 people

INGREDIENTS

- 2 Salbei leaves
- 2 Thymian branches
- 1 Lemon
- 5.5 oz fresh spring onions
- Extra virgin olive oil
- Salt
- 7 oz Plaice Fillets
- Black pepper
- 1 Rosemary branch

METHOD

1. Cut off the ends of the spring onions, then slice them thinly and wash them under water.
2. Now take a baking dish, add oil, salt and pepper and mix everything well. Set aside. Chop the sage, thyme and rosemary with a knife. Slice the lemon very thinly.
3. Brush a baking sheet with olive oil. Place the Schollenfilets on it and season with pepper, salt and chopped herbs. Place the spring onions and lemon slices between each fillet. Bake at 390°F for 20 minutes.
4. Now serve and enjoy!

Cod Burger

Difficulty level: easy
Preparation: 16 min
Cooking time: 11 min
Servings: 2 Stück

INGREDIENTS

- 12 oz Cod Fillet
- 1 tablespoon grated thyme
- 1 tablespoon grated lemon zest
- 1 tablespoon chopped parsley
- 1/4 tsp black pepper
- 1/4 tsp salt
- 1/4 cup breadcrumbs
- 1/4 cup wheat flour
- 1 egg
- 1/4 tsp black pepper
- 1/4 tsp salt
- Sunflower oil

METHOD

1. Rinse the cod fillets and dry them thoroughly, then debone them using kitchen tweezers.
2. Chop the fillets into small pieces so that they can be processed into a homogeneous paste in a food processor.
3. Place the fish paste in a bowl, add pepper, salt, chopped parsley, grated lemon zest, and thyme. Stir to combine all the flavors.
4. Use a round mold with a diameter of about 3 inches, to shape the fish burger. Place half of the mixture in the first mold, press down to shape the burger. Remove the mold and repeat the process for the second burger.
5. Whisk the egg in a bowl with pepper and salt.
6. Dredge the burgers first in flour, then in the egg, and finally in breadcrumbs.
7. Heat the oil in a pan to about 350°F, fry the burgers in it for 4 minutes on each side.
8. Once the burgers are cooked, remove them from the pan and place them on paper towels to drain excess oil.

Veal with Vegetables

Difficulty level: very easy
Preparation: 11 min
Cooking time: 16 min
Servings: 2 people

INGREDIENTS

- 7 oz Kalbfleisch (beef) in slices
- 2 tablespoons soybean sprouts
- 1.75 oz red onions
- 3.5 oz green beans
- 1.75 oz yellow peppers
- 1.75 oz red peppers
- 2 tablespoons cashews
- 1.5 tablespoons soy sauce
- 3 tablespoons extra virgin olive oil
- 2 tablespoons wheat flour
- Salt

METHOD

1. Wash the red pepper and cut it in half, remove the inner threads and seeds. Then cut it into thin strips. Repeat the same process with the yellow pepper.
2. Remove the end of the spring onion, remove the outer layer and chop it finely.
3. Wash the beans, remove the ends and cut them into diamond shape.
4. Heat a wok on high flame, add one tablespoon of oil and fry the cashews for 60 seconds. Remove the cashews.
5. Pour in another tablespoon of oil and add all the previously cut vegetables. Add salt and stir fry for about ten minutes on high flame.
6. Slice the beef slices into about 0.8 inch wide strips.
7. Take a bowl and mix flour and salt together, put the meat in the bowl and flour it well.
8. After the vegetables have been cooked for 10 minutes, remove them from the wok and set them aside.
9. Now add another tablespoon of oil and add the beef strips. Cook for a few minutes and then add the soy sauce in the wok.
10. Add a little water in the wok so that a thick, creamy consistency is formed.
11. Use the entire sauce that has formed during cooking, to serve.

Seafood Skewers

Difficulty level: easy
Preparation: 21 min
Cooking time: 11 min
Servings: 4 Stück

INGREDIENTS

- 9 oz cleaned squid
- 5.5 oz cuttlefish (about 4)
- 4 shrimp
- 4 tomatoes
- 1.5 tablespoons white wine
- 1 tablespoon extra virgin olive oil
- Salt
- 2 tablespoons breadcrumbs
- 1 tablespoon extra virgin olive oil
- 2 tablespoons chopped parsley
- 1 garlic clove
- Black pepper

METHOD

1. Clean the cuttlefish thoroughly.
2. Cut the cuttlefish in the middle of the bag so that you can open it and cut it into rectangular pieces.
3. Cut the squid into strips that are not wider than a few centimeters.
4. Also clean the shrimp by removing the head and shell. Remove the gut (the black thread on the shrimp's back).
5. Cut the cherry tomatoes in half.
6. Alternately thread cuttlefish and squid onto skewers, then half a cherry tomato, a shrimp and cuttlefish and again squid. Close the skewer with another cherry tomato half.
7. Repeat the process for all skewers.
8. Mix breadcrumbs with parsley, garlic, pepper and some oil.
9. Dip the skewers on both sides in the breadcrumbs.
10. Heat a pan with a few tablespoons of extra virgin olive oil on high heat. Cook the skewers for 5/6 minutes, turn the skewers and cook for an additional 5 minutes.

Chicken Cutlets with Balsamic Vinegar

Difficulty level: easy
Preparation: 21 min
Cooking time: 11 min
Servings: 2 people
Hinweis: mehr als 1 Stunde Ruhezeit zum Marinieren

INGREDIENTS

- 9 oz chicken breast
- 1.75 oz extra virgin olive oil
- 1 tablespoon lemon liqueur
- 1 tablespoon balsamic vinegar
- Juice of half a lemon
- 2 bay leaves
- 1 garlic clove
- 1 sprig thyme
- 1 sprig rosemary
- Black pepper
- Salt

METHOD

1. Prepare a bowl with olive oil and the juice of half a lemon. Add rosemary, bay leaves, thyme, balsamic vinegar and lemon liqueur. Mix everything thoroughly.
2. Remove the fat from the chicken breast and then cut it into about 0.5 inch thick slices.
3. Dip the slices in the bowl with all the aromas. Turn them over to flavor them on all sides. Cover the bowl with plastic wrap and place it in the refrigerator for at least 1 hour.
4. Take a pan and pour in some oil, let the oil drain and add a garlic clove. Fry the garlic for about 30 seconds, then remove it and add the chicken slices.
5. Turn them over so that both sides are well fried.

Shrimp with Coconut Aroma

Difficulty level: easy
Preparation: 21 min
Cooking time: 11 min
Servings: 2 people

INGREDIENTS

- 18 oz shrimp
- 2.75 oz coconut flour
- 2.75 oz rice flour
- 2 eggs
- Salt
- 3.5 oz sunflower oil
- 2 oz soy milk
- 1.5 teaspoon tomato paste
- 1.5 teaspoon lime juice
- 0.2 tablespoons red curry
- Salt
- 35 oz peanut oil

METHOD

1. Place sunflower oil, lime juice, and soy milk in a blender. Add salt and blend until the mixture is thick. Divide the sauce into 3 bowls.
2. Leave one bowl unseasoned.
3. In the second bowl, add tomato paste and stir thoroughly.
4. In the third bowl, add red curry and mix.
5. Clean the shrimp: remove the head, legs, and gut on the back.
6. Take 3 baking dishes and fill them as follows: rice flour, beaten eggs, coconut flour. Salt the beaten eggs.
7. The shrimp go through this process: first flouring, then dipping in beaten eggs, and then in coconut flour.
8. Heat the peanut oil in a pot and bring the oil to a temperature of about 350°F.
9. Dip the shrimp one by one and fry them for 1 minute.
10. Drain the shrimp and let them dry on absorbent paper.
11. Serve the fried shrimp with the 3 sauces prepared earlier.

Flavored Sliced Beef

Difficulty level: easy
Preparation: 6 min
Cooking time: 9 min
Servings: 2 people

INGREDIENTS

- 9 oz beef sirloin
- Extra virgin olive oil
- Black pepper
- Salt
- 2 sprigs of marjoram
- 2 sprigs of rosemary
- 2 sprigs of thyme
- 4 sage leaves

METHOD

1. Take a slice of beef sirloin about 1.6 inches thick.
2. Prepare the spices: place rosemary needles, marjoram, sage leaves, thyme, and parsley on a cutting board and finely chop.
3. Hold the meat in a bowl with salt, black pepper, and olive oil and mix all ingredients in the bowl. Spread the spices on both sides of the meat slice.
4. Heat a stovetop over high flame and sprinkle coarse salt over it. Place the meat slice only on the hot stovetop and cook it for about 4 minutes per side, keeping the inside pink.
5. When the meat is cooked, place it on a cutting board and slice it into about 0.4 inches thick slices.

Sliced Beef with Balsamic Vinegar

Difficulty level: easy
Preparation: 6 min
Cooking time: 11 min
Servings: 2 people

INGREDIENTS

- 14 oz beef tenderloin
- Salt
- Black pepper
- 2 tablespoons extra virgin olive oil
- 4 juniper berries
- 8.5 oz balsamic vinegar
- 2 cinnamon sticks

METHOD

1. Remember to take the meat out at least 1 hour before cooking (you'll get a better dish then).
2. Heat the balsamic vinegar in a small pot over low heat and add the cinnamon and juniper berries. Cook until the sauce is reduced by half, then strain the sauce through a sieve.
3. Heat a grill pan over high heat with two tablespoons of olive oil. Once the grill pan is very hot, grill the meat for about 2 minutes on each side, keeping the inside pink and season it on both sides with salt and pepper.
4. Slice the meat into 1 inch thick slices and drizzle the meat with the balsamic vinegar sauce.

Chicken Skewers

Difficulty level: easy
Preparation: 21 min
Cooking time: 11 min
Servings: 2 people

INGREDIENTS

- 14 oz chicken breast
- 4.5 oz zucchini
- 2.75 oz mushrooms
- 12 thin slices of smoked bacon (4.2 oz)
- 2 sprigs of rosemary

METHOD

1. Cut the chicken breast into about 1.2 inch cubes, making 12 cubes.
2. Wash the zucchini, remove the two ends and slice them into about 0.4 inch thick slices (12 slices).
3. Also slice the mushrooms into 0.4 inch thick slices (12 slices).
4. Break the rosemary into 12 equal pieces.
5. Wrap a slice of bacon around each chicken cube. Thread the coated nut onto a skewer. Add the zucchini slice and mushroom slice onto the skewer.
6. Repeat the process a total of 12 times.
7. Now heat a grill plate generously and put the skewers in. Cook over medium heat so that the bacon gradually melts, turn all skewers constantly and cook for about 15 minutes.

Beef Slices with Tomato

Difficulty level: easy
Preparation: 6 min
Cooking time: 11 min
Servings: 2 people

INGREDIENTS

- 4 slices of beef (12 oz)
- 4.5 oz canned tomatoes
- 2 tablespoons extra virgin olive oil
- 1 tablespoon butter
- 1 shallot
- 1 garlic clove
- 1 sprig of marjoram
- 1 sprig of thyme
- Black pepper
- Salt

METHOD

1. Chop the shallot. Heat a pan with oil and butter, add the previously crushed garlic and chopped shallot and cook for fifteen minutes.
2. Add the meat to the pan and brown on both sides, then add thyme and marjoram. Now add the canned tomatoes and cook for 5 minutes over high flame, after 5 minutes season with salt and pepper.
3. Serve the slices drizzled with their own juices.

Fried Chicken Wings

Difficulty level: easy
Preparation: 21 min
Cooking time: 11 min
Servings: 6 Stück

INGREDIENTS

- 6 Chicken Wings
- 1 teaspoon sweet paprika
- 1 teaspoon dried thyme
- 1 tablespoon chopped parsley
- 2 tablespoons wheat flour
- 1 egg
- Peanut oil
- Black pepper
- Salt

METHOD

1. Beat the egg in a bowl with salt and pepper.
2. Clean the chicken skin and then remove the hair with a kitchen tweezers, if possible, otherwise, you will burn them with the fire of the stove. Rinse the cleaned chicken wings thoroughly and then dry them carefully with kitchen paper.
3. Take a bowl and mix in it: flour, salt, pepper, chopped parsley, thyme, and paprika.
4. Put the chicken wings now in the bowl with the beaten egg and then dip them in the bowl with the seasoned flour, to coat them with breadcrumbs.
5. Heat plenty of oil in a large pan. Test the temperature by letting some flour crumbs fall into the oil: when they start to fry, the temperature is fine.
6. Dip in a few chicken wings now (if the size of the pan allows it).
7. Fry each pair of wings for 10 minutes, of course, turning them a few times.
8. Let the chicken wings drain on a layer of paper towels.

Currywurst

Difficulty level: easy
Preparation: 11 min
Cooking time: 21 min
Servings: 2 people

INGREDIENTS

- 2 veal bratwurst
- 1 tablespoon curry powder
- 1/2 cup canned diced tomatoes
- 1/2 cup ketchup
- 2 teaspoons curry powder
- 1 teaspoon paprika
- 1 teaspoon sweet paprika
- 1 onion
- 2 cups hot water
- Extra virgin olive oil
- Salt
- 1/2 lb sweet potatoes
- 1/2 lb potatoes
- Salt
- Oil

METHOD

1. Finely chop the onion and sauté in a pan with some oil for 30 seconds. Then add the paprika, ketchup, and diced tomatoes and let the sauce simmer. Add the curry powder, season with salt and add two cups of hot water. Cook until you get a thick cream.
2. Peel the sweet potatoes and cut them into about 0.5 inch wide and 2.75 inch long sticks.
3. Peel the potatoes and cut them into thin slices to make chips.
4. Heat the oil to about 350°F and fry first the classic chips and then the sweet chips. Drain on a layer of paper towels.
5. Boil a pot of water with a spoonful of curry powder and add the sausages. Cook for about 6 minutes and then drain and cook them for another minute on a hot plate to make them crispy.
6. Serve the sausages with the prepared sauce and French fries.

Spicy Sausages

Difficulty level: very easy
Preparation: 11 min
Cooking time: 21 min
Servings: 2 people

INGREDIENTS

- 8 oz sausages
- 1 garlic clove
- 1 bay leaf
- 1 sprig rosemary
- Extra virgin olive oil
- Black pepper
- Salt

METHOD

1. If the sausages are tied together with a string, you can divide them.
2. Heat some oil in a pan and brown the sausages together with the garlic, rosemary, and bay leaf.
3. Cook the sausages for 10 minutes and turn them as soon as they start to brown on the side. After 10 minutes, remove the garlic, rosemary, and bay leaf, reduce the heat, and cook for an additional 10 minutes covered.

Pan-Seared Sole with Butter and Sage

Difficulty level: easy
Preparation: 16 min
Cooking time: 11 min
Servings: 2 people

INGREDIENTS

- 2 medium-sized sole fillets
- 3 oz butter
- 6 sage leaves
- All-purpose flour
- Black pepper
- Salt

METHOD

1. Clean, skin and wash the sole and dry them thoroughly.
2. Dredge the sole on both sides in flour.
3. Melt the butter in a pan with the sage leaves, add the sole to the pan and cook for about 4 minutes on each side.
4. Once cooked, season with salt and pepper and pour the melted butter, which has remained in the pan, over the sole.

Burger-Trio

Difficulty level: very easy
Preparation: 21 min
Servings: 3 patties

INGREDIENTS

- 6.5 oz ground beef
- Black pepper
- Salt
- 6.5 oz ground beef
- 1 sprig rosemary
- 1 sprig thyme
- 4 sage leaves
- Black pepper
- Salt
- 5 oz ground beef
- 1.75 oz Edam cheese
- Black pepper
- Salt

METHOD

1. Divide the ground beef into 3 bowls (A. 6.3 oz + B. 6.3 oz + C. 5.8 oz)
2. In bowl A, add salt and pepper and mix with your hands.
3. Prepare a sheet of parchment paper and place a round mold with a diameter of about 4 inches on top, pour the contents of bowl A into it and press it evenly, then remove the mold.
4. Finely chop the rosemary, thyme, and sage and add them to bowl B. Mix with your hands.
5. Use the mold again and shape the second meat patty on the parchment paper.
6. Grate the Edam cheese into large flakes and add it to bowl C, season with salt and pepper and mix with your hands.
7. Use the mold again and shape the third meat patty on the parchment paper.
8. Now the burger-trio is ready to cook!

Veal with Saffron

Difficulty level: easy
Preparation: 6 min
Cooking time: 11 min
Servings: 2 people

INGREDIENTS

- 12 oz slices of veal
- 2 cups vegetable broth
- 1/2 cup cream
- 2 tablespoons all-purpose flour
- 1/4 teaspoon saffron (1 packet)
- Chopped parsley
- Extra-virgin olive oil
- Salt

METHOD

1. Pound the veal slices and season with salt. Dust both sides with flour and keep them aside.
2. Heat the vegetable broth in a pot and add the saffron packet to infuse the flavor.
3. Now heat some oil in a pan, add the veal slices and brown them on high heat for 2/3 minutes per side. Then add the vegetable broth and cream, turn the heat down and simmer for 5 minutes with a lid on.
4. After 5 minutes, remove the lid, turn the heat up and cook further until the sauce thickens. Then you can turn off the heat and serve with chopped parsley.

Aromatized Beef

Difficulty level: very easy
Preparation: 11 min
Cooking time: 11 min
Servings: 2 people

INGREDIENTS

- 1 pound beef sirloin (4 slices)
- 1 tablespoon extra virgin olive oil
- 2 tablespoons butter
- 2 sprigs thyme
- All-purpose flour
- Black pepper
- Salt

METHOD

1. Pound the beef slices.
2. Melt the butter in a pan with the thyme sprigs.
3. Dust the beef slices with flour on both sides and place them in the pan.
4. Cook on medium heat for about 5 minutes, then flip the slices and cook for an additional 2 minutes on medium heat, to allow the sauce to thicken.
5. Season with salt and pepper before serving.

Plaice meatballs

Difficulty level: easy
Preparation: 16 min
Cooking time: 12 min
Servings: 8 pieces

INGREDIENTS

- 13.25 oz herbs
- 4 oz Plaice fillets
- 2 oz cow milk ricotta
- 1.5 tablespoons bread crumbs
- 2 strands of chives
- 1 clove of garlic
- Extra virgin olive oil
- Salt
- 1.5 tablespoons bread crumbs

METHOD

1. Bring a pot of water to a boil, add the Schollenfilets and cook for 1 minute, drain and chop with a knife.
2. Carefully drain the Schollen meat and put it in a bowl with the ricotta, chop the chives and add them to the bowl, then season and mix all the ingredients well.
3. Now you can prepare the meatballs, we recommend about 1 tablespoon per piece. Once they are ready, dip them all in 1.5 tablespoons of bread crumbs to make the coating.
4. Cut the stems of the herbs and wash them.
5. Heat a pan with olive oil and garlic, add the still moist herbs and fry them for about 5 minutes over medium heat.
6. After 5 minutes you can turn off the heat.
7. Now heat a little oil in another pan and fry the patties for about 5 minutes.
8. When all the ingredients are cooked, you can serve them by arranging a layer of herbs and placing the patties on top.

Wrapped Sausages

Difficulty level: very easy
Preparation: 16 min
Cooking time: 11 min
Servings: 2 people

INGREDIENTS

- 2 sausages
- 3.5 oz bread dough

METHOD

1. Divide the bread dough into two pieces, about 1.8 oz each, and roll it out into a rectangle large enough to wrap around the sausage.
2. Now wrap the sausage completely in the dough.
3. Cut the surface of the dough crosswise.
4. Bake at 390°F for 10 minutes.

Swordfish Tartar

Difficulty level: very easy
Preparation: 16 min
Servings: 2 people

INGREDIENTS

- 5.5 oz swordfish fillet
- 2.75 oz cherry tomatoes
- 2.25 oz extra virgin olive oil
- 1 tablespoon shallot
- 0.5 tsp parsley
- 0.5 tsp basil
- 0.5 tsp marjoram
- 0.5 tsp capers
- 1 lemon
- 0.5 tsp mint
- Black pepper
- Salt

METHOD

1. Finely chop the shallot and capers. Do the same with the parsley, basil, marjoram, and mint.
2. Grate the lemon zest and reserve it, then squeeze the lemon juice into a container. Add salt, pepper and oil. Use a blender to puree everything.
3. Cut all cherry tomatoes into 4 pieces so you can remove the seeds, then cut them into small cubes.
4. Take the swordfish fillet and remove the outer skin. Cut the fillet into small cubes as well.
5. Mix: swordfish, cherry tomatoes, herbs, capers, and lemon zest.
6. Place the tartar on a plate and serve with the lemon cream.

Bites of Pollock

Difficulty level: very easy
Preparation: 6 min
Cooking time: 6 min
Servings: 2 people

INGREDIENTS

- 7 oz Pollock fillets
- 1.5 tablespoons butter
- 1.5 oz whole, peeled hazelnuts
- 3 sage leaves
- 1 lime
- Black pepper
- Salt

METHOD

1. Cut each fillet into 3 or 4 pieces to make bite-sized pieces.
2. Keep the fish in the refrigerator while you continue with the rest of the recipe.
3. Add the hazelnuts to a pan and fry them for about 5 minutes on a low flame. After 5 minutes, remove the hazelnuts and set aside to cool.
4. In the same pan, melt the butter with the sage leaves. Once the butter is melted, add the Pollock pieces and grate half of the lime zest over them.
5. Squeeze the lime into the pan and season with salt and pepper.
6. Now turn the heat to medium to high and cook the morsels for 5 minutes, turning them occasionally with tongs.
7. Now the Pollock is ready to serve, so take a spoon and put the morsels on the plates. Pour the boiling broth over them.
8. Chop the hazelnuts with a knife and sprinkle the crumbs over the Pollock. Grate the last half of the lime zest and the dish is ready to serve!

Pork with Roquefort

Difficulty level: easy
Preparation: 16 min
Cooking time: 11 min
Servings: 2 people

INGREDIENTS

- 14.25 oz pork loin
- 2 tablespoons butter
- 4 sage leaves
- 4 slices of bacon
- Extra virgin olive oil
- Salt
- 2.5 tablespoon Roquefort (or Gorgonzola)
- 4.5 oz heavy cream
- Salt

METHOD

1. Cut the pork loin into 2 fillets, each weighing 7 oz.
2. Place one slice of bacon on each fillet, place a sage leaf on each side of the fillets and then wrap them with another slice of bacon.
3. Tie the fillets with kitchen twine so they don't open during cooking.
4. Pour oil and butter into a pan and fry them for 30 seconds on low heat.
5. Now you can add the fillets and cook them on medium heat for 5 minutes per side.
6. Cut the Roquefort (or Gorgonzola) cheese into small pieces.
7. When the fillets have cooked for 5+5 minutes, remove them from the pan and keep them separate. In the same pan, bring the heavy cream and cheese to a simmer on medium heat and thicken while stirring slowly.
8. When you have a homogeneous cream, you have all the ingredients ready.
9. Arrange the fillets on plates and drizzle the fresh cheese over them.

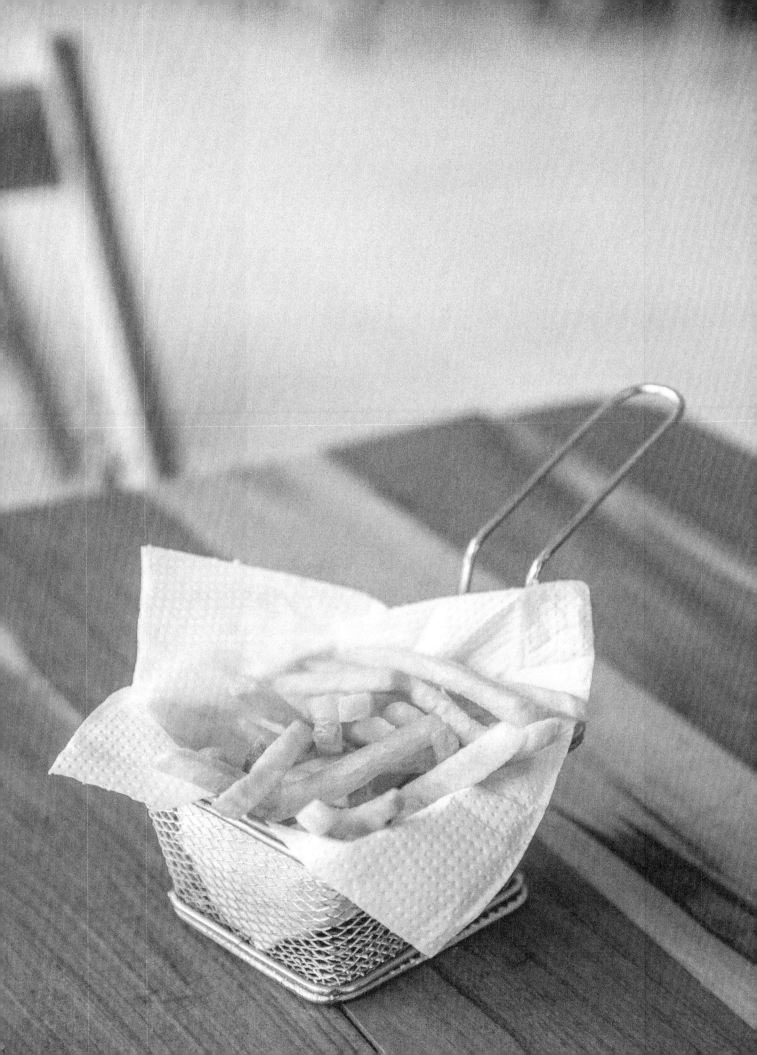

SIDE DISHES

Pan-Fried Fennel

Difficulty level: very easy
Preparation: 6 min
Cooking time: 12 min
Servings: 2 people

INGREDIENTS

- Thyme
- 16 oz fennel (about 2)
- Marjoram
- 1 tablespoon extra virgin olive oil
- Himalayan salt
- Pink pepper

METHOD

1. Take the fennel, wash it and cut off the bottom and the stems. Then cut them into wedges.
2. Take a pan, heat some olive oil and add the fennel. Cook on medium heat for 6 minutes.
3. Generously salt the fennel with Himalayan salt (this type of salt gives color but has less flavor compared to regular salt).
4. Add marjoram leaves to the pan and cook for another 6 minutes.
5. Serve hot!

Grilled Oyster Mushrooms

Difficulty level: very easy
Preparation: 16 min
Cooking time: 6 min
Servings: 2 people

INGREDIENTS

- 1 teaspoon apple cider vinegar
- Salt
- 11.5 tablespoons oyster mushrooms
- 2 tablespoons extra virgin olive oil
- 1 teaspoon lemon zest
- 3 mint leaves
- 1.5 teaspoon lemon juice
- Arugula
- Thinly sliced lemons

METHOD

1. Take the mushrooms and make sure to clean them thoroughly from dirt. Separate the stems with a knife from the caps. Set aside.
2. Add lemon juice, extra virgin olive oil, a pinch of salt, lemon zest and finally the three chopped mint leaves in a bowl. Mix well and set aside to flavor the mushrooms.
3. Heat the grill, place the mushrooms on it and grill for a few minutes on both sides until cooked through.
4. Arrange the mushrooms on a plate and dress with the prepared dressing, garnish with arugula and lemon slices.
5. Serve hot.

French Fries

Difficulty level: very easy
Preparation: 11 min
Cooking time: 16 min
Servings: 2 people

INGREDIENTS

- 14.25 oz potatoes
- Salt
- 12.5 oz peanut oil for frying

METHOD

1. Take the potatoes and peel them. Cut them into 0.5 inch thick slices and give them the classic french fry shape.
2. Take a pan and heat the oil. Once it reaches 320°F, drop in a few potatoes at a time.
3. After 6 minutes, or when they are golden brown, remove them from the hot oil and place them on absorbent paper towels. This will remove excess oil.
4. Serve the french fries hot and well salted, or with some sauce!

Rosemary Roasted Pumpkin

Difficulty level: easy
Preparation: 11 min
Cooking time: 16 min
Servings: 2 people

INGREDIENTS

- 14.25 oz pumpkin flesh
- 1.75 oz white wine
- 2 tablespoons extra virgin olive oil
- 1 garlic clove
- Salt
- 1 sprig rosemary
- Black pepper

METHOD

1. First, take the pumpkin, remove the skin and cut the pumpkin flesh into small pieces (the size of walnuts).
2. Take a frying pan, add some oil and fry a garlic clove. Once it is golden brown, remove it with tongs.
3. Add the pumpkin pieces and fry them.
4. Cook the pumpkin for 11 minutes and stir it in the pan. Season with pepper and enjoy!

Cauliflower puree

Difficulty level: very easy
Preparation: 16 min
Cooking time: 16 min
Servings: 2 people

INGREDIENTS

- 1.5 tablespoons Grana Padano PDO for grating
- 1.25 lbs Potatoes
- 1/2 Garlic clove
- 1.5 lbs Cauliflower
- Nutmeg
- Coarse Salt, 1/2 tsp
- Water
- Salt
- Extra virgin olive oil
- Black pepper

METHOD

1. Clean the vegetables. Remove the outer leaves of the cauliflower and the stem. Wash the cauliflower heads well and place them on kitchen paper.
2. In the meantime, take the potatoes and remove the peel. Slice them into slices according to your taste.
3. Now take the pressure cooker, add a little oil and half a chopped garlic. Add the potatoes and cauliflower florets. Pour water into the pressure cooker until it is at the same level as the vegetables. Add 1 tsp of coarse salt. Cook the potatoes and cauliflower. When you hear the pressure cooker whistle, set the timer for 6 minutes.
4. Remember to let the steam escape from the pressure cooker before opening it!
5. If you do not have a pressure cooker, cook the two vegetables separately for 40 minutes. The vegetables should be very soft.
6. Now take the blender and put it in the pot. Mix all ingredients well until a homogeneous cream is formed.
7. Season with salt and pepper, grate some nutmeg and add, mix for 4 minutes.
8. Pour the cream into a bowl and grate some Grana Padano cheese on the surface, so that it is completely covered. Place the bowl at 450°F with the grill function for about 6 minutes in the oven (or until the cheese is golden and crispy) and a crust forms.

Roasted Broccoli

Difficulty level: very easy
Preparation: 11 min
Cooking time: 21 min
Servings: 2 people

INGREDIENTS

- 9 oz Broccoli
- 5.5 oz Water
- 1 tablespoon Extra virgin olive oil
- 1 Garlic clove
- 1 Fresh chili pepper
- Salt

METHOD

1. Take the broccoli and remove the stems. Wash the heads in fresh water. Take a pot, pour in some water, add the broccoli, cover it with a lid and bring the water to a boil.
2. Then cook for an additional 11 minutes, add some salt and let all the water evaporate.
3. Chop the garlic and chili pepper, add the olive oil and pour it into the pan. Let it cook for 3 minutes.
4. Now put everything into a bowl and serve the broccoli hot or cold!

Roasted Soybean Sprouts

Difficulty level: very easy
Preparation: 6 min
Cooking time: 7 min
Servings: 2 people

INGREDIENTS

- 7 oz Soybean sprouts
- 1 tablespoon fresh ginger
- 1 fresh chili pepper
- 1.5 teaspoon oil
- 1.5 tablespoons soy sauce
- 1.5 teaspoon water

METHOD

1. First, take the ginger and peel it, then cut it into very thin slices. Take the chili pepper and cut it into small rings.
2. Take the wok and heat it on high flame. Once it is hot, pour in some oil, add the chili and ginger.
3. Once they are well browned, add the soybean sprouts and stir-fry for a few minutes. Continuously stirring, add some soy sauce and water, a total of about 7 minutes.
4. Pour them into a bowl and enjoy!

Fried Mushrooms

Difficulty level: very easy
Preparation: 21 min
Cooking time: 4 min
Servings: 2 people

INGREDIENTS

- 4.5 oz Champignons
- 4 oz Shiitake mushrooms
- 4 oz Cremini mushrooms
- 3.5 oz Water
- 35 oz Peanut oil
- Salt
- 2.75 oz Breadcrumbs
- 2.75 oz All-purpose flour

METHOD

1. Clean the mushrooms first. Take the shiitake mushrooms, wash them well and separate the stem with a knife from the cap. After washing the mushrooms, cut them in half lengthwise. After washing the cremini mushrooms, cut them in half lengthwise.
2. Prepare the batter now. Take a bowl, add the flour in it and gradually add the water, mixing it well with a whisk until a smooth mixture is formed. Then add the salt.
3. Take another bowl, add some breadcrumbs in it and set it aside.
4. Now take a pan and add the peanut oil in it to fry the mushrooms.
5. While the oil is heating, take the mushrooms, dip them in the batter, let them drip a little and then dip them in the breadcrumbs.
6. When the oil is hot, add the mushrooms in and turn them occasionally so they are well fried on both sides.
7. Place them on a plate with paper towels, season them with salt and serve them hot!

Fried Artichokes with Mustard

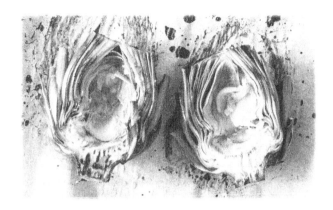

Difficulty level: easy
Preparation: 21 min
Cooking time: 6 min
Servings: 2 people

INGREDIENTS

- Salt
- 1 medium egg
- Instant yeast
- 4 artichokes
- 1/4 cup all-purpose flour
- 1/2 tsp mustard powder
- Peanut oil

METHOD

1. Take the artichokes and remove the harder outer leaves. Cut through the top with a knife so that the thorns are removed. Cut off the stem so that at least 1 inch of the base of the artichoke remains. To prevent them from wilting, squeeze half a lemon over them.
2. Now that the artichokes are clean, cut them into 8 pieces, immediately submerge them in warm water and add the remaining lemon juice.
3. Let's prepare the dough. Place the flour, salt, mustard, olive oil, and yeast in a bowl. Mix all ingredients together well with a mixer. If the dough is too liquid, add a little more flour. If the dough is too thick, add a little water.
4. Take a pan and add the peanut oil to fry the mushrooms.
5. While the oil is heating up, take the mushrooms, dip them in the dough and let them drain a bit.
6. When the oil is hot, add the mushrooms and turn them from time to time to brown them evenly, about 6 minutes.
7. Place them on a plate with paper towels, season with salt and serve hot!

Seasoned Carrots

Difficulty level: easy
Preparation: 11 min
Cooking time: 21 Minuten
Servings: 2 people

INGREDIENTS

- 1/2 tsp black pepper
- 1/4 tsp cinnamon powder
- 1/4 tsp nutmeg
- 1 tbsp extra virgin olive oil
- 1 bay leaf
- 2 juniper berries
- 1 clove
- 9 oz baby carrots
- 1 pinch of cardamom
- Salt

METHOD

1. Wash the baby carrots. Cut off the ends with a knife.
2. Take the steamer and fill it halfway with water, heat it up and add the bay leaves.
3. Add the pepper, juniper berries, cloves and cardamom seeds.
4. When the water is boiling, put the steamer basket on the steamer to heat it up. When it's hot, place the carrots on top of the basket. Cover with a lid for 20 minutes.
5. When the carrots are done, serve them on a plate and season them with salt and pepper. Add a drizzle of extra virgin olive oil and some nutmeg and cinnamon.

Roasted Brussels Sprouts

Difficulty level: very easy
Preparation: 6 min
Cooking time: 21 min
Servings: 2 people

INGREDIENTS

- Salt
- 2 oz bacon
- 9 oz Brussels sprouts
- 1/2 cup vegetable broth
- 3/4 oz diced shallot
- Black pepper
- 1 tsp extra virgin olive oil

METHOD

1. Heat the vegetable broth in a pot. Meanwhile, wash the Brussels sprouts, drain them, and remove the outer leaves. Cut them in half. Take the bacon and cut it into strips.
2. Heat a pan with oil and add the diced shallot. When they are golden brown, add the bacon strips and cook for 3 minutes.
3. Add the Brussels sprouts, salt, pepper and vegetable broth. Cook with a lid for 14 minutes. When they are finished, drain them and enjoy them hot!

Microwave potatoes

Difficulty level: very easy
Preparation: 6 min
Cooking time: 8 min
Servings: 2 people

INGREDIENTS

- Salt
- 1 tbsp water
- 7 oz potatoes
- 1 sprig rosemary
- Extra virgin olive oil

METHOD

1. Peel potatoes of the same size (small to medium).
2. Place them in a bowl, add water and the rosemary sprig.
3. Cover with plastic wrap and microwave at 900 W for 8 minutes.
4. At the end of 8 minutes, test with a skewer if the potatoes are soft inside and season with salt and oil.
5. Serve and enjoy hot!

Potatoes and Peppers

Difficulty level: very easy
Preparation: 11 min
Cooking time: 21 min
Servings: 2 people

INGREDIENTS

- 1.5 lbs potatoes
- 2.5 oz native olive oil extra
- 5.5 oz yellow pepper
- 5.5 oz red pepper

METHOD

1. Wash the potatoes well and cut them into 0.5 inch thick slices. Wash, clean and cut the peppers into thin slices. Add everything to a bowl.
2. Take a large frying pan and heat some native olive oil. Once hot, add the potatoes and peppers.
3. Season with salt and pepper as it cooks and stir occasionally to ensure the vegetables cook evenly.
4. After 21 minutes, the potatoes should be golden brown. Then serve and enjoy!

Fried Zucchini

Difficulty level: very easy
Preparation: 16 min
Cooking time: 5 min
Servings: 2 people
Note: 2 hours rest time for the zucchini

INGREDIENTS

- 1 lb (16 oz) Zucchini
- 2 tsp coarse salt
- 1/4 cup wheat flour
- 1 1/4 cups peanut oil

METHOD

1. Wash the zucchini, cut off the ends, and slice them into about 1/4 inch thick slices.
2. In a bowl, prepare a bed of coarse salt and lay the zucchini slices on top. Crush the zucchini with another plate to release any excess water. Let the zucchini sit for 2 hours.
3. After 2 hours, rinse the zucchini and place them in a bowl with the flour. Toss to coat the zucchini evenly. Shake off any excess flour.
4. Heat the oil in a pan. Once hot, add the zucchini slices and fry for 5 minutes, or until golden brown.
5. Remove the zucchini from the oil and place them on paper towel to remove any excess oil.
6. Serve hot and crispy.

Fried Cauliflower

Difficulty level: very easy
Preparation: 16 min
Cooking time: 16 min
Servings: 2 people

INGREDIENTS

- 1.5 lbs Blumenkohl
- 1 tablespoon Sardellen in Öl
- Natives Olivenöl extra
- 1.5 oz entsteinte schwarze Oliven
- Salt
- Black pepper
- 1 garlic clove
- Parsley

METHOD

1. Wash the salt from the capers and soak them in a bowl of cold water.
2. Take the cauliflower, remove the outer leaves, cut off the florets and wash them well. Boil the florets for 6 minutes, drain and set aside. Take a non-stick skillet, add some oil and fry a garlic clove.
3. Once the garlic is golden brown, add the cauliflower florets and season with salt and pepper. Stir well and cook for 3 minutes over medium heat. Now add the washed and set aside capers, the black olives and the anchovies.
4. Turn the flame to high and fry all the ingredients for about 6 minutes to mix well.
5. Transfer to a bowl and serve hot with chopped parsley!

SALADS

Artichoke Salad

Difficulty level: easy
Preparation: 31 min
Servings: 2 people

INGREDIENTS

- 3 Artichokes
- 1.5 tablespoons Grana Padano cheese
- 1 Lemon
- 1 tablespoon Lemon juice
- Salt
- Black pepper
- 2 tablespoons Extra virgin olive oil

METHOD

1. Take the artichokes and remove the tougher outer leaves. Then cut through the top with a knife to remove the thorns. Cut off the stem so that at least 1 inch of the base of the artichoke remains. To keep them fresh, squeeze half a lemon over them.
2. Halve the artichoke and remove the inner fuzz, then slice the artichoke into thin slices. As you slice the artichoke, soak the slices in a bowl of water with lemon. When you are done, pour off the excess water, let the artichoke slices drain, and set them aside.
3. Now take the Grana Padano cheese, slice it into thin slices and set it aside.
4. Take a bowl, squeeze 1 tablespoon of lemon juice and mix it with 1.06 oz of extra virgin olive oil, add pepper and salt, and mix the ingredients into a sauce.
5. Take a bowl, add the artichokes, previously prepared sauce, and Grana Padano shavings. Finish the garnish with a drizzle of olive oil.
6. Enjoy this simple but delicious salad!

Chickpea Salad

Difficulty level: very easy
Preparation: 31 min
Servings: 2 people

INGREDIENTS

- 2 tablespoons extra virgin olive oil
- 1/3 cup cooked chickpeas
- 1/4 cup red onions
- Black pepper to taste
- 1/4 cup diced cucumbers
- 1/2 cup diced yellow bell peppers
- 1 teaspoon mint
- 1/2 cup diced zucchini
- 1/4 cup diced tomatoes
- 1/4 cup crumbled feta cheese
- 1 lemon
- Salt

METHOD

1. Wash and dry the vegetables thoroughly.
2. Dice the bell peppers and discard the seeds.
3. Halve the cherry tomatoes.
4. Remove the ends of the zucchini and slice them into thin rings.
5. Remove the ends of the cucumber and slice them into thin rings.
6. Slice the onions into thin rings.
7. Crumble the feta cheese.
8. Set the vegetables aside and prepare the dressing. In a blender, combine the mint leaves, extra virgin olive oil, and lemon juice. Blend well and transfer to a bowl.
9. Drain the cooked chickpeas and add them to the bowl with the other vegetables. Toss well with the mint dressing, add a squeeze of lemon juice, and sprinkle the crumbled feta cheese on top.
10. Serve and enjoy!

Salad with Chicken and Zucchini

Difficulty level: very easy
Preparation: 16 min
Cooking time: 16 min
Servings: 2 people
Hinweis: 1 Stunde zum Marinieren des Hähnchens

INGREDIENTS

- 7 oz chicken breast sliced
- 3.5 oz zucchini
- Salt
- 2.5 tablespoon mixed greens
- 3.5 oz eggplant
- Extra virgin olive oil
- 2.5 oz cherry tomatoes
- 1 tablespoon wildflower honey
- Salt
- 1 tablespoon extra virgin olive oil
- Juice of half a lemon
- Thyme
  - Black pepper

METHOD

1. Start with the chicken by making small cuts on both sides of the slices to allow the marinade to penetrate well. Take a baking dish, add some olive oil and place the chicken breasts in it. Now add the honey, salt, pepper, juice of half a lemon and one or two sprigs of thyme. Toss the chicken well so that the spices penetrate. Cover everything with plastic wrap and let it rest for about an hour.
2. Now move on to the vegetables. Wash and slice the zucchini into about 0.5 inch thick strips. Do the same with the eggplant. Take the cherry tomatoes and cut them into four pieces.
3. Heat the grill, grease it with a little oil and grill the eggplant and zucchini by turning them on both sides. Season with salt.
4. Take the marinated chicken that was set aside and grill it on both sides.
5. Let the vegetables and chicken cool and put everything in a bowl.
6. Now that the salad is ready, you can enjoy it with whatever you like!

Salad with Pears, Arugula, Parmesan and Walnuts

Difficulty level: very easy
Preparation: 11 min
Servings: 2 people

INGREDIENTS

- 1 Williams-pears
- 1/4 cup grated Grana Padano
- 2 tablespoons extra-virgin olive oil
- Salt
- 2 cups arugula
- 1 tablespoon balsamic vinegar
- 1/4 cup chopped walnuts

METHOD

1. Wash and dry the arugula and place it in a bowl.
2. Wash the pear, peel it and remove the core. Slice it into thin slices.
3. Chop the walnuts coarsely.
4. Add the pears to the bowl with the arugula, add the grated Parmesan cheese, season with oil, salt, and vinegar and mix the ingredients well.
5. Sprinkle the salad with chopped walnuts and enjoy!

Salad with Pears and Gorgonzola Cheese

Difficulty level: very easy
Preparation: 11 min
Servings: 2 people

INGREDIENTS

- 1/2 cup chopped Walnuts
- 1 lb Kaiser Pears
- Salt
- Extra virgin Olive oil
- 2 cups Spinach
- Balsamic Vinegar
- 1/2 lb cooked Beets
- 4 oz Gorgonzola cheese

METHOD

1. Wash the pears, remove the core and cut them into 1 1/2 inch pieces. Set them aside.
2. Cut the cooked beets into 3/4 inch pieces.
3. Finely chop the walnuts.
4. Form small Gorgonzola cheese balls using a teaspoon.
5. In a bowl, combine the spinach, pears, beets, and Gorgonzola cheese balls. Season with olive oil, balsamic vinegar, and salt.
6. Enjoy your salad now!

Cucumber Salad

Difficulty level: very easy
Preparation: 16 min
Servings: 2 people

INGREDIENTS

- 1/4 cup red onions
- 1/2 cup cherry tomatoes
- 1 cup cucumbers
- 1/4 cup spinach
- 1/2 cup yellow cherry tomatoes
- 1 tablespoon apple cider vinegar
- 1/4 cup Greek yogurt
- Black pepper
- 1 tablespoon extra virgin olive oil
- Salt

METHOD

1. Wash and thinly slice the spring onions, place in a bowl with water and ice, set aside.
2. Cut the yellow and red cherry tomatoes into quarters.
3. Peel the cucumbers, slice the outer parts into long, thin strips.
4. The middle part of the cucumber is too soft due to the seeds, so cut this part into cubes.
5. In a container, add the cucumber cubes. Add oil, salt, pepper, apple cider vinegar, and Greek yogurt. Blend all ingredients in a blender until smooth.
6. On a plate, add spinach leaves as the base for the salad, then add the dried onions, the colorful cherry tomatoes and finally the cucumber strips.
7. Now take the yogurt sauce and pour over your salad!

Salad with Sardines, Cherry Tomatoes and Eggs

Difficulty level: very easy
Preparation: 21 min
Cooking time: 8 min
Servings: 2 people

INGREDIENTS

- 2 Eggs
- Extra Virgin Olive Oil
- Black Pepper
- Salt
- 5.5 oz. Head Lettuce
- 2 oz. Pitted Black Olives
- 4.5 oz. Cherry Tomatoes
- 1 tablespoon. Sardines in Oil
- 2.5 oz. Tuna
- 1.5 tablespoons. Fresh Spring Onions

METHOD

1. Start by preparing the hard-boiled eggs. Take the eggs, put them in a pot and pour water over them until they are covered.
2. After 7 minutes of cooking time, drain the eggs and cool them in cold water.
3. Now take the spring onions, remove the green part and slice them thinly.
4. Take the cherry tomatoes and cut them into four pieces.
5. Drain the sardine fillets and cut them into small pieces.
6. Take the eggs, peel them, cut them as desired and set them aside.
7. Wash the head lettuce, cut it into pieces and put it in a bowl.
8. Add the tomatoes, sardine fillets, black olives, tuna and spring onions and season with oil, salt and pepper. Finally, put the eggs on top so they don't fall apart.
9. Enjoy your salad!

Apple-Chicken Salad

Difficulty level: very easy
Preparation: 11 min
Cooking time: 16 min
Servings: 2 people

INGREDIENTS

- 4 oz apples
- 1 pomegranate
- Black pepper
- 12 oz chicken breast
- 2.5 tablespoon arugula
- 2.5 tablespoon spinach
- Salt
- 1 tablespoon mustard
- 1.5 teaspoon apple cider vinegar
- 2 tablespoons extra virgin olive oil
- Black pepper
- Salt

METHOD

1. Slice the chicken breast into about 0.4 inch thick slices.
2. Take a baking dish, add a little oil and place the chicken on it, season it with salt and pepper. Set aside to let the spices marinate.
3. Wash the arugula and spinach, dry the leaves well and set them aside.
4. Take the pomegranate and remove only the red part, you need 2.6 oz.
5. Place the grill plate on the stove and grill the chicken for 5 minutes on each side, once it's hot. Once the chicken is cooked, set it aside.
6. Prepare the sauce in a bowl. Pour in the mustard, add apple cider vinegar, extra virgin olive oil, pepper and salt.
7. Wash, dry and slice the apples into thin slices. Don't forget to remove the core!
8. Now take the chicken and slice it into diagonal strips.
9. Assemble the salad by starting with the arugula and spinach, add the apple slices and chicken and finish with the mustard sauce.

Salad with Tuna, Carrots, Corn and Green Beans

Difficulty level: very easy
Preparation: 16 min
Cooking time: 8 min
Servings: 2 people

INGREDIENTS

- 9 oz green beans
- Salt
- 6.25 oz carrots
- 4 oz tuna in oil with lemon and black pepper
- 2.75 oz corn
- 1 tablespoon chopped chives

METHOD

1. Pour water into a pot and bring it to a boil.
2. Meanwhile, wash and dry the green beans, cut off the ends and put them in boiling water for 8 minutes. Drain them as soon as they are done and put them in a bowl with ice to keep them crisp. After cooling, drain them and put them in a separate bowl.
3. Take the carrots, peel them and cut them as desired.
4. Cut the chives.
5. Drain the corn and season the tuna with lemon and black pepper.
6. Now take the bowl with the green beans, add the corn, tuna, carrots and chives.
7. Now take the balsamic vinegar, put it in a bowl, add oil, salt and a splash of water.
8. Just before serving, dress the salad with the balsamic vinegar sauce and enjoy!

Crispy Salad

Difficulty level: easy
Preparation: 16 min
Cooking time: 6 min
Servings: 2 people

INGREDIENTS

- 1 tablespoon chopped parsley
- 1 small head of iceberg lettuce
- 1.5 oz Parmesan cheese in flakes
- Salt
- Black pepper
- Extra virgin olive oil
- 1 carrot
- 4 anchovy fillets
- 2 sandwich slices
- White wine vinegar

METHOD

1. Wash the iceberg lettuce, finely chop it and put it in a salad bowl.
2. Peel the carrots and cut them as desired.
3. Take the Parmesan cheese and slice it.
4. Finely chop the parsley and anchovy fillets.
5. Take a bowl and add oil, salt, pepper, anchovy fillets, parsley and a drop of vinegar. Mix the ingredients together and let them stand for a few minutes.
6. Remove the dark edges of the bread slices and cut the center into cubes. Take a frying pan, add some oil and fry the bread cubes.
7. Take the salad bowl with the iceberg lettuce, add the carrots, the Parmesan shavings, the oil dressing with the anchovies and the parsley. Mix well.
8. Finally, add the croutons and serve the salad!

ONE-PLATE MEALS

Classic Sandwich

Difficulty level: easy
Preparation: 19 min
Cooking time: 9 min
Servings: 1 Sandwich

INGREDIENTS

- 5.5 oz Turkey cutlets
- 3.5 oz Auburn-Tomatoes
- 2 slices of bacon (2 tablespoons total)
- 3 slices of white bread
- 2 leaves of lettuce
- 1 tablespoon Butter
- 2 tablespoons Mayonnaise

METHOD

1. Butter the 3 slices of bacon evenly with a knife and then fry them for a few minutes on each side in a pan.
2. Once the slices are crispy, set them aside on paper towel to drain.
3. Now, fry the turkey cutlets for a few minutes on each side and set them aside when they are done.
4. Wash the tomatoes and slice them thinly, then wash and dry the lettuce leaves.
5. Spread one side of each slice of bread with mayonnaise. On the side of the bread with mayonnaise, place the lettuce, followed by two slices of turkey, two slices of tomato, and one slice of bacon. Close the sandwich with one slice of bread, with the mayonnaise facing the bacon.
6. The first layer of the sandwich is done!
7. Now, spread mayonnaise on the sandwich and place the lettuce, chicken, tomato and bacon on top.
8. Cut the sandwich in half and serve it!

Tacos

Difficulty level: very easy
Preparation: 14 min
Cooking time: 14 min
Servings: 4 Stück

INGREDIENTS

- 9 oz Wurst
- 4 Tacos
- 1.5 teaspoon natives Olivenöl extra
- 1.5 teaspoon sweet chili
- 1 tablespoon tomato paste
- 1 tablespoon smoked paprika
- Black pepper
- 2.75 oz cherry tomatoes
- 1.5 tablespoons spring onions
- juice of half a lime
- 1.5 teaspoon natives Olivenöl extra
- 1 bundle parsley
- Salt
- Peel of half a lime
- 2 tablespoons Greek yogurt
- 2 oz sour cream

METHOD

1. Remove the skin from the sausage and crumble the meat with a fork. Remove the chili pepper, wash it, and remove all seeds from the inside, then slice it into thin strips.
2. Add oil to a non-stick pan, heat it quickly on medium flame, and add the sausage and paprika. After a few minutes, add the chili pepper.
3. Add a pinch of pepper and the tomato paste. Cook for 15 minutes, stirring the ingredients.
4. Meanwhile, prepare the salad: wash and cut the tomatoes, remove the roots of the spring onions, and slice them into thin strips. Wash and chop the parsley with a knife. Take a bowl and mix all salad ingredients with extra native olive oil, some salt and lime juice.
5. Prepare the sauce by mixing the yogurt, sour cream, and lime peel well.
6. Turn off the pot with the meat and fill the tacos.
7. Take the tacos, place the sausage on the bottom, then add the tomato and spring onion salad, and finally season with a spoonful of yogurt sauce.
8. And now enjoy your tacos!

Croque Madame

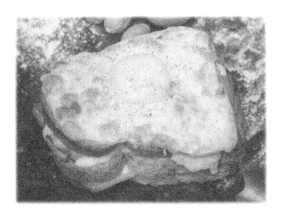

Difficulty level: easy
Preparation: 9 min
Cooking time: 9 min
Servings: 2 pieces

INGREDIENTS

- 8 tablespoons butter
- 1.5 ounces Gruyère
- 2 medium eggs
- 4 sandwich slices
- 1.5 ounces cooked ham
- Salt

METHOD

1. Take 4 tablespoons of butter, melt it in a pot and spread it on all bread slices. Grate the Gruyère and place it along with the cooked ham on the bread slices. Close with another bread slice.
2. Take 4 tablespoons of butter and melt it in a skillet over low heat, then place the sandwich in until it is crispy on both sides. Take a 4 inch diameter ring mold and place it in a hot skillet with butter. Crack an egg into it. Cover the skillet with a lid to ensure the egg cooks through. (Repeat for the other egg.)
3. When the egg is ready, carefully place it on the crispy sandwich and serve it hot!

Spicy Sandwich with Tuna, Olive Pesto and Goat Cheese

Difficulty level: very easy
Preparation: 11 min
Servings: 2 Stück

INGREDIENTS

- 4 leaves of baby lettuce
- 3.5 oz of tuna in oil with chili
- 2 hard wheat rolls
- 1.5 oz of goat cheese
- 1 medium Auburn tomato (1.6 oz)
- 2 tablespoons of pitted Taggiasca olives
- 1 tablespoon of extra virgin olive oil

METHOD

1. Let's start preparing the olive pesto. Put the pitted Taggiasca olives in a bowl, add oil and blend with a hand blender until a cream is formed.
2. Take the sandwiches, divide them in half and spread one side of the slices with the freshly made olive cream and the other half with the goat cheese.
3. Wash the lettuce and place the leaves on the sides where the olive cream is.
4. Take the tomato, wash it and cut it into thin slices, then place it on the lettuce leaf.
5. Now open the can of chili-tuna and let the preserving oil drain off. Place it on the tomato slices and close the sandwich with the roll halves, where you spread the goat cheese.
6. Serve and enjoy!

Piadine with Corn and Chicken

Difficulty level: easy
Preparation: 11 min
Cooking time: 18 min
Servings: 2 people

INGREDIENTS

- 2 Piadine
- 1/2 teaspoon Sweet Paprika
- 1/2 teaspoon Black Pepper
- 1/2 teaspoon Garlic Powder
- 9 oz Chicken Breast
- 1/2 teaspoon Dried Onion
- 1/2 teaspoon Dried Thyme
- 1/2 teaspoon White Pepper
- 1 Bay Leaf
- Salt
- 7 oz canned yellow corn kernels
- 1 tablespoon extra virgin olive oil
- Juice of half a lemon
- 1 fresh chili pepper
- 3.5 oz Greek yogurt
- Salt

METHOD

1. First, grind all the spices in a blender.
2. Take the chicken breasts, wash them well, remove the fatty parts and cut them into 5 pieces. Then cover them with the spice powder obtained earlier.
3. Take a frying pan, heat two tablespoons of oil and put in the chicken pieces. Fry the chicken on both sides well done and then set it aside to rest.
4. Meanwhile, take the corn and remove the liquid. Season the corn with lemon juice and chopped chili (make sure it has no seeds!).
5. Take the Greek yogurt and mix it well.
6. Now quickly heat the Piadina, they must remain soft so they can close.
7. Spread the Greek yogurt well on the hot Piadina, slice the chicken into thin strips and place them along with the corn in the center of the Piadina.
8. Now starting from the bottom, roll up the Piadina, serve and enjoy it warm!

Couscous with Feta, Watermelon, and Tomatoes

Difficulty level: very easy
Preparation: 26 min
Cooking time: 6 min
Servings: 2 people

INGREDIENTS

- 4.5 oz Feta
- Extra virgin olive oil
- 5.5 oz yellow, red, and green tomatoes
- 5.5 oz Couscous
- 2.75 oz Watermelon fruit flesh
- Oregano
- Salt
- Black pepper

METHOD

1. Boil some water in a pot where you will cook the couscous.
2. Take a bowl, add the couscous and season it with oil and salt. Slowly pour the boiling water into the bowl until the couscous is covered.
3. Take the plastic wrap and cover the bowl for about 6 minutes.
4. Meanwhile, take the watermelon, remove the skin and cut the fruit flesh into small cubes (less than 0.4 inches).
5. Take the feta and cut it into cubes the size of the watermelon. Cut the cherry tomatoes into wedges.
6. Take the couscous, add a little oil, mix it well with a spoon and add salt.
7. Add the watermelon, feta, and cherry tomatoes to a bowl. Season with oil, salt, pepper, and oregano.
8. Cut the remaining watermelon for decoration into long, thin triangles.
9. Take the pastry ring and place the couscous on a plate. Remove the ring and place the feta, cherry tomatoes, and watermelon on top.
10. Use your imagination and garnish the dish to your taste!

Piadina with Gorgonzola, Prosciutto and Tomatoes

Difficulty level: very easy
Preparation: 11 min
Cooking time: 6 min

INGREDIENTS

- 2 classic Piadine
- 7 oz. of beefsteak tomatoes
- 7 oz. of creamy Gorgonzola
- 8 Slices of Prosciutto
- Salt

METHOD

1. Wash the tomatoes and slice them into thin slices.
2. Take a non-stick pan and heat it up, then add the tomato slices.
3. Sauté the tomato slices on both sides and then set them aside to rest.
4. Take a frying pan, add some oil and quickly fry the Piadina on both sides.
5. Place the Piadina on a plate, spread one side with Gorgonzola, add the tomatoes, and place 2 slices of Prosciutto on top. Halve and serve hot!

Piadina with Stracchino Cheese and Zucchini

Difficulty level: easy
Preparation: 6 min
Cooking time: 26 min
Servings: 1 Person

INGREDIENTS

- 4.25 oz Stracchino
- 1 Piadina
- 2 tablespoons Walnuts
- 7 oz Zucchini
- Balsamic Vinegar Glaze
- Salt

METHOD

1. Chop the walnuts and set them aside.
2. Wash the zucchini well and slice it thinly (about 0.12 inches). Place them on the heated grill for 2 minutes, then flip them over and wait for another 2 minutes. Set them aside and season them with some salt.
3. Take a non-stick pan and place the Piadina on it, heat it for 30 seconds and then flip it for another 30 seconds. While the Piadina is still in the pan, add the Stracchino to one side, cover the pan and let the cheese melt. Place the Piadina on a plate, add the chopped zucchini and walnuts and drizzle some balsamic vinegar over it. Enjoy it warm!

Double Cheeseburger

Difficulty level: easy
Preparation: 14 min
Cooking time: 13 min
Servings: 2 burgers

INGREDIENTS

- 1 lb ground beef
- 4 slices of cheddar cheese
- 1/2 cup grated carrots
- 1/2 cup salad greens
- 1 tablespoon mayonnaise
- 1 tablespoon ketchup
- Worcestershire sauce
- 1 tomato
- 4 slices of pickled jalapeño peppers
- Baby spinach
- Extra virgin olive oil
- Salt
- Black pepper

METHOD

1. Take the salad greens, wash them, discard the center part and slice the rest into thin strips. Peel the carrots and grate them coarsely.
2. Take a bowl and add the mayonnaise, ketchup, salad greens, and carrots. Add a small spoonful of Worcestershire sauce and a pinch of pepper. Mix well.
3. Take the meat and shape it into two burgers about 0.75 inch tall. Season both sides with salt and pepper. Take a non-stick pan, add a little oil and heat it well.
4. Add the burgers to the pan and cook for 4 minutes per side over medium heat. Once all sides are cooked, reduce the heat, place a slice of cheddar on one side and cover the pan with a lid.
5. Once the cheese is melted, place one burger on top of the other. In the meantime, heat the two bread halves in a toaster.
6. Place the double burgers on a plate and prepare the double cheeseburger sandwich.
7. Start with the bread, then add the sauce with salad and carrots, the meat, two slices of jalapeños, two leaves of baby spinach, and two tomato slices.
8. Close the sandwich and serve it warm!

Mozzarella and Tomato Omelette

Difficulty level: easy
Preparation: 9 min
Cooking time: 9 min
Servings: 1 Stück

INGREDIENTS

- 2 eggs
- 1 tomato
- 3.5 oz. mozzarella cheese
- Salt
- Black pepper
- Basil
- Extra virgin olive oil

METHOD

1. Cut the mozzarella into cubes and pat it dry with paper towels to remove any excess moisture.
2. Wash the tomatoes and slice them into equal sized rounds.
3. Take a frying pan and heat the tomato slices on both sides, then set them aside.
4. Crack two eggs into a bowl, add salt and pepper and whisk with a whisk.
5. Take a frying pan and add some oil, heat it well, add the eggs and place a lid on the pan.
6. When it starts to boil, add the tomatoes and the mozzarella on one side. Add two fresh basil leaves.
7. Fold the omelet into a half moon shape, continue to cook and flip it so that the mozzarella melts.
8. Once melted, serve it on a plate and enjoy it hot!

Bowl with Quinoa, Cheese, Apple and Red Fruits

Difficulty level: very easy
Preparation: 16 min
Cooking time: 11 min
Servings: 2 people

INGREDIENTS

- 3.5 oz Quinoa
- 7 oz Apples
- 1.5 oz Appenzeller cheese
- 1 Avocado
- 2 tablespoons Whole, peeled hazelnuts
- 1 tablespoon Pumpkin seeds
- 1 tablespoon Raspberries
- 1 Branch of currants
- Chives

METHOD

1. Rinse the quinoa under water and then cook it in boiling salted water for the time specified on the package.
2. While the quinoa is cooking, take a pan and roast the hazelnuts for a few minutes and then set them aside.
3. Take the cheese, remove the rind, and cut it into cubes.
4. Cut the chives with a knife.
5. Halve the avocado, remove the skin and pit, and slice the flesh into thin slices.
6. Take the apples, wash them, and cut them into squares about 0.4 inches.
7. When all the ingredients are ready, take the bowls and add the quinoa first, then the avocado, laying it on its side and forming a pattern with the apple squares.
8. Then distribute the raspberries, pumpkin seeds, and the currant branch around the edges of the bowls. Garnish with chives and the previously roasted hazelnuts.
9. Serve and enjoy!

Bowl with Salmon, Crispy Bread, and Avocado

Difficulty level: easy
Preparation: 11 min
Cooking time: 16 min
Servings: 2 people

INGREDIENTS

- 6 oz salmon
- 3.5 oz Basmati rice
- 1 avocado
- 1.5 tablespoons whole grain bread
- 1/2 lemon
- 1 tablespoon extra virgin olive oil
- Poppy seeds
- Thyme
- Salt
- Black pepper

METHOD

1. Cook the Basmati rice for 10 minutes in boiling water.
2. Cut the whole grain bread into 0.5 inch cubes. Place the cubes on a baking sheet with extra virgin olive oil and bake in a preheated oven at 390°F for 9 minutes. When the bread is crispy, remove from the oven and let it cool.
3. Take a pan and add 2 teaspoon of olive oil, place the salmon in it and add salt, pepper, and thyme. Cook for 7 minutes until the salmon forms a crispy layer.
4. Take the avocado, remove the skin and stone. Cut the flesh into small cubes.
5. Drain the rice and distribute it into bowls.
6. Take the lemon and cut it into thin slices, removing the peel.
7. Start assembling the bowls and place the avocado, salmon, and crispy bread as desired. Finally, sprinkle with lemon and poppy seeds.
8. Serve the bowls and enjoy!

Tuna and Zucchini Carpaccio

Difficulty level: easy
Preparation: 11 min
Servings: 2 people
Hinweis: 30 Min. zum Marinieren der Zucchini

INGREDIENTS

- 5.5 oz drained tuna in oil
- 7 oz zucchini
- 2 tablespoons extra virgin olive oil
- 2.75 oz mozzarella balls
- 2.75 oz cherry tomatoes
- Parsley
- 2 tablespoons lemon juice
- Zest from half a lemon
- Mint
- Salt
- Black pepper

METHOD

1. Open the tuna can, drain all the oil and transfer to a bowl. Set aside.
2. Wash the zucchini and slice it into very thin rounds.
3. Wash the lemon, zest it and slice the zest into thin strips (make sure not to cut the white part, which is bitter). Juice the remaining half of the lemon, strain it and pour it into a bowl. Add some oil, salt and pepper. Chop the parsley and mint with a knife and add to the lemon juice. Mix well with a fork.
4. Pour some of the seasoned lemon juice into a baking dish and place a layer of zucchini on top. Pour the remaining juice over the zucchini. Cover the zucchini with plastic wrap and let it marinate in the refrigerator for 30 minutes.
5. While the zucchini is marinating, wash the tomatoes, cut them as desired and add them to a bowl with oil and salt.
6. Now let's serve! Take the marinated zucchini and place a few slices on the plate, add the mozzarella, tomatoes and tuna.
7. Enjoy your meal!

Quinoa Eggplant and Mint

Difficulty level: very easy
Preparation: 16 min
Cooking time: 11 min
Servings: 2 people

INGREDIENTS

- 3.5 oz Quinoa
- 4.5 oz Eggplants
- 1.5 teaspoon extra virgin olive oil
- 4.5 oz Cherry Tomatoes
- 2 tablespoons Feta
- 2 tablespoons Red Onions
- Mint
- 1.5 tablespoons Water
- 1 tablespoon Arugula
- Black Pepper
- Salt

METHOD

1. Take the eggplants, wash them, and cut them into cubes.
2. Wash the cherry tomatoes and cut them into 4 pieces. Cut the red onions into slices, prepare a pan with extra virgin olive oil and put the onions on it. Cook on medium to high heat. I recommend adding a splash of water and stirring so that the onions fry and don't burn.
3. After about 5 minutes, add the eggplants and cherry tomatoes and season with salt and pepper.
4. Let it cook for another 6 minutes and stir occasionally. After turning off the flame, season with mint leaves.
5. Now take the quinoa and wash it. Cook it in boiling water according to the time indicated on the package. Once the quinoa is cooked, drain it and let it cool.
6. Let's serve!
7. Take a clear glass to show the layers of ingredients. Place the quinoa on the bottom, then the eggplants and then the cherry tomatoes. Place the diced feta and a few leaves of arugula on the cherry tomatoes!
8. Now you just have to enjoy the dish!

Tacos with Shrimp and Kale

Difficulty level: easy
Preparation: 16 min
Cooking time: 16 min
Servings: 2 Stück

INGREDIENTS

- 2 Corn Tortillas
- 4.5 oz Kale
- 4.25 oz Cooked red beans (drained)
- 1 tablespoon Shrimp
- 1 Garlic Clove
- Zest of 1 Lemon
- 1 Fresh chili
- 1.5 tbsp Extra virgin olive oil
- 1 tablespoon Hot water
- Fine salt, 1/2 tsp
- 2.75 oz Greek yogurt
- Extra virgin olive oil, 1/2 tbsp
- Acacia honey, 1/2 tsp
- Chives

METHOD

1. Let's start with the shrimp. Remove the shells from the tails and make sure to remove the black thread.
2. Place them in a bowl and season with oil, salt, and lemon zest. Mix well, cover with plastic wrap and let it rest in the refrigerator.
3. Take the kale, wash it, and slice it into very thin slices.
4. Take a pan now, add oil, one garlic clove, and a chopped chili pepper.
5. When the pan is hot, add the kale, add water, and stir well for it to take on flavor. Cover with a lid and cook for 9 minutes.
6. Remove the garlic when the kale has wilted and add the drained red beans. Mix all ingredients well.
7. Now we are going to make the sauce. Take a bowl and add chopped chives, yogurt, honey, and a little salt. Stir well to mix the ingredients. Set aside.
8. Take the shrimp out of the refrigerator and heat them in a frying pan for 1 minute on each side and set aside. Turn off the flame of the kale.
9. Take a frying pan and heat the tortilla.
10. Place the tortilla on a plate, add the kale and beans, then add the shrimp and season well with the sauce.
11. Enjoy warm!

DESSERTS

Hot Chocolate

Difficulty level: very easy
Preparation: 11 min
Cooking time: 6 min
Servings: 1 Person

INGREDIENTS

- 1 tablespoon unsweetened cocoa powder
- 1 tablespoon sugar
- 9 oz whole milk
- 1 tablespoon cornstarch
- 2.25 oz dark chocolate (60-69%)

METHOD

1. Cut the dark chocolate into small pieces and place in a bowl to heat in a double boiler over medium heat. Stir the chocolate as it melts and set aside.
2. In a small saucepan, combine the milk, cornstarch, and unsweetened cocoa powder. Heat and stir with a whisk, adding the sugar.
3. Pour in the melted chocolate and continue stirring until desired consistency is reached.
4. Serve with a dollop of whipped cream or fruit of your choice!

Candied Almonds

Difficulty level: easy
Cooking time: 14 min
Note: There is a cooling time

INGREDIENTS

- 2.25 oz sugar
- 4.5 oz almonds
- 1.5 tablespoons water

METHOD

1. In a saucepan, combine the almonds, sugar, and water at room temperature.
2. Turn heat to medium-low and stir ingredients. Once the sugar forms a coating around the almonds, reduce heat and continue stirring until the sugar takes on a amber color.
3. Line a baking sheet with parchment paper and place the almonds in a circular pattern.
4. Allow to cool and enjoy!

French Toast

Difficulty level: very easy
Preparation: 12 min
Cooking time: 6 min
Servings: 7 Stücke

INGREDIENTS

- 2 fl oz whole milk
- 7 slices brioche
- Ground cinnamon
- 2 medium eggs
- Salt
- Butter
- Ground cinnamon
- Blueberry jam
- Butter

METHOD

1. In a large casserole dish, beat the eggs and add them along with the milk, cinnamon, and a pinch of salt. Mix the ingredients well.
2. Take the brioche slices and place them in the casserole dish, soaking both sides.
3. Now melt some butter in a pan, place the bread slices on it, and fry for 3 minutes on each side. While you are frying the brioche slices, set them aside.
4. Garnish the bread slices with a little butter, a pinch of cinnamon, and some blueberry jam. You can adjust the recipe to your taste.
5. Now they are ready to be enjoyed!

Pancakes

Difficulty level: very easy
Preparation: 6 min
Cooking time: 11 min
Servings: 6 pieces

INGREDIENTS

- 2 tbsp sugar
- 2 tsp baking powder
- 1 cup (8 fl oz) whole milk
- 1 cup (5 oz) all-purpose flour
- 1 tbsp butter
- 1/4 cup (2 tablespoons) blueberries

METHOD

1. In a bowl, mix together the flour, baking powder, and sugar.
2. Melt a small amount of butter in a pan over low heat. Once melted, remove from heat and set aside.
3. Pour the milk into the flour mixture slowly, whisking to avoid clumps. Add the melted butter and whisk until well combined.
4. Heat a nonstick pan over medium heat. Spoon a ladleful of the batter into the center of the pan.
5. Watch the batter. When it forms many bubbles, flip the pancake with a spatula to the other side. Repeat this process for all the pancakes.
6. Blend the blueberries with a hand blender, adding a small amount of water and a pinch of sugar.
7. Place the pancakes on a plate, pour the blueberry sauce over them, and sprinkle with powdered sugar!

Cake in a Cup

Difficulty level: easy
Preparation: 9 min
Cooking time: 1 min
Servings: 2 people
Note: Microwave is essential

INGREDIENTS

- 1/4 cup Sunflower oil
- 2 tablespoons unsweetened cocoa powder
- 1/2 cup sugar
- 2/3 cup all-purpose flour
- 1 egg
- 1/4 cup whole milk
- 1.5 oz white chocolate, chopped
- 1 teaspoon baking powder

METHOD

1. Take the egg, add sugar, and beat with an electric mixer until a white foamy mixture forms.
2. Sift the cocoa, flour, and baking powder into a separate bowl and mix well. Slowly add this mixture to the bowl with the foamy egg and pour in the milk.
3. Mix well to avoid lumps, and add a little oil.
4. Process the ingredients until they are smooth and homogeneous.
5. Take a cup and pour the mixture into it, leaving about 1 inch from the rim.
6. Add the chopped white chocolate and cover the cup with microwave-safe plastic wrap.
7. Set the microwave to 600 watts and cook for about 2-3 minutes.
8. Take the cup and let it cool.
9. Meanwhile, beat the cream with a whisk and add it to the cooled cupcake.
10. Enjoy!

Yogurt Pancakes

Difficulty level: very easy
Preparation: 11 min
Cooking time: 2 min
Servings: 2 people
Note: Let the batter rest for 30 minutes

INGREDIENTS

- 1 medium egg
- 2.25 oz fat-free yogurt
- 1.5 teaspoon baking powder
- 2.75 oz wheat flour
- 3.5 oz whole milk
- Extra virgin olive oil

METHOD

1. Take a bowl and beat the egg with a whisk until it's light and frothy.
2. Add the milk and yogurt to the mixture, continuing to stir.
3. In a separate bowl, sift the flour and add the baking powder.
4. Slowly mix the two mixtures until a smooth, homogeneous batter is formed. Cover with plastic wrap and let it rest for 30 minutes.
5. Take a non-stick pan and lightly oil it with extra virgin olive oil, pour the batter into the center:
6. Watch the batter. When many bubbles have formed, flip the pancake with a spatula to the other side. Repeat this process for all pancakes.
7. Serve the pancakes with chocolate, cream or fruit to your taste!

Berry Yogurt Cup

Difficulty level: easy
Preparation: 11 min
Cooking time: 1 min
Servings: 2 people
Note: Cooling time in refrigerator about 19 minutes

INGREDIENTS

- 1 cup Greek yogurt
- 1 tablespoon honey
- 1/2 cup berries
- 1/2 cup crunchy cereal
- 2 teaspoons sugar
- 1 tablespoon water
- 1 teaspoon cornstarch

METHOD

1. Take a small saucepan, add water, sugar, and berries (save a few for garnish) and heat over low heat.
2. Let sit for 6 minutes. When the berries have fallen apart, strain the mixture through a sieve to make it smooth and seedless.
3. Dissolve 2 teaspoons cornstarch in a little water and add to the berry mixture. Let it stand on the stove so that it thickens well.
4. Pour the thickened mixture into 2 glasses and let them stand in the refrigerator for 19 minutes. In the meantime, take the yogurt and add 1 tablespoon honey and stir well.
5. Take the two glasses out of the refrigerator and pour the yogurt in. Add a layer of crunchy cereal and garnish with the berries set aside earlier.
6. Now you just have to enjoy them!

Tiramisu Truffles

Difficulty level: very easy
Preparation: 11 min
Servings: 15 pieces
Note: Allow to rest in the freezer (20 minutes)

INGREDIENTS

- 4.5 oz Mascarpone
- 3 oz ladyfingers
- 1.5 oz coffee (at room temperature)
- 2 tablespoons powdered sugar
- Unsweetened cocoa powder

METHOD

1. Prepare the coffee, approximately 1.4 oz, and let it cool.
2. Crush the ladyfingers into a powder.
3. Add the Mascarpone to a bowl, pour in the cooled coffee and powdered sugar. Stir well to create a homogeneous mixture.
4. Add the crushed ladyfingers and continue to work the mixture until it is fairly compact.
5. Take a spoon, scoop some of the mixture and shape it into a ball. Repeat this process until the mixture is done.
6. Pour the unsweetened cocoa powder into a bowl. Roll each ball in the bowl of unsweetened cocoa.
7. Allow to rest in the freezer for 30 minutes.
8. Now serve and enjoy these delicious tiramisu truffles!

Waffles

Difficulty level: easy
Preparation: 6 min
Cooking time: 5 min
Servings: 2 people
Note: The dough must rest for 30 minutes. Waffle iron required.

INGREDIENTS

- 5.5 oz all-purpose flour
- 2 oz butter
- 1.5 oz sugar
- 1 vanilla bean
- 1.5 teaspoon baking powder
- 4.5 oz whole milk
- 1 egg
- A pinch of salt
- Powdered suga

METHOD

1. Take a bowl and beat the egg, gradually add the milk and melted butter. Mix the ingredients well and add the sugar. Sift the flour, baking powder, and salt and mix all the ingredients in the bowl with the milk and eggs.
1. Now add the inside of the vanilla bean and add it to the batter, cover it with plastic wrap and let it rest in the refrigerator for 30 minutes.
2. Heat the waffle iron to maximum temperature and brush it with some melted butter so that the batter does not stick.
3. Take a scoop of the mixture and pour it over. Close the waffle iron and bake for about 4 minutes, until the mixture is golden brown.
4. The waffle should be crispy on the outside but soft on the inside.
5. Serve it with powdered sugar and anything you like! Chocolate, cream, fruits, and much more!

Oatmeal with Hazelnuts and Apples

Difficulty level: easy
Preparation: 6 min
Cooking time: 4 min
Servings: 1 Person

INGREDIENTS

- 1/2 oz hazelnuts
- 1 apple
- 1 1/2 tbsp acacia honey
- 2 1/2 oz oatmeal
- 1/3 cup whole milk
- 4 oz water
- A pinch of cinnamon powder
- A pinch of salt

METHOD

1. Take a pot and pour in some water, milk, and a pinch of salt, then add the oatmeal and stir well. Turn the heat to medium to low.
2. Cook the porridge for about 5 minutes until it is creamy and thick. Turn off the heat, add a pinch of cinnamon and stir well.
3. Pour the mixture into a bowl and set aside.
4. Meanwhile, take the apples, wash them and cut them into very thin rings.
5. Take a pan and pour in some honey, let it heat for 2 minutes then add the apples. Heat each side for 1 minute.
6. Take the bowl with the porridge and start to garnish it! Start with the apple slices, add hazelnuts and a pinch of cinnamon and drizzle with honey.
7. And now, enjoy!

Chia Pudding

Difficulty level: easy
Preparation: 11 min
Servings: 1 Person
Note: Let sit in the refrigerator for one night

INGREDIENTS

- Mint (for decoration)
- 1 tablespoon Chia seeds
- 1 tablespoon Greek yogurt
- 1 tablespoon Almond milk
- 0.5 tsp Unsweetened cocoa powder
- 1.5 teaspoon Heather honey
- 1.5 oz Cherries in syrup

METHOD

1. Take a bowl and add the chia seeds, add the unsweetened cocoa powder, pour in some almond milk while stirring.
2. Continue until the mixture is smooth.
3. Add the heather honey to the mixture, stir, and cover the bowl with plastic wrap.
4. Let it sit in the refrigerator overnight.
5. Take a clear glass to see the layers! Spoon the mixture on the bottom, then the yogurt, then the cherries in syrup and start over!
6. Decorate with a few cherries and mint!

Cappuccino Milkshake

Difficulty level: very easy
Preparation: 11 min
Servings: 2 people

INGREDIENTS

- 2 cups coffee
- Ice
- 1/2 cup whole milk
- 2 tablespoons sugar
- 1 teaspoon unsweetened cocoa powder
- Whipped cream
- 5 coffee beans
- Unsweetened cocoa powder

METHOD

1. Make a cup of coffee with the espresso machine. Take a pot and heat up the milk, 2 tablespoons sugar, the coffee, and the cocoa, stirring well.
2. Take the blender, add in the ice, and add the liquid from the pot. Blend everything on the highest setting until you get a creamy consistency.
3. Serve the milkshake in two chilled glasses and garnish it with cocoa powder, coffee beans, whipped cream, or chocolate shavings!

Chocolate Cup with Mascarpone and Meringues

Difficulty level: very easy
Preparation: 16 min
Servings: 2 people
Note: Resting time in the refrigerator

INGREDIENTS

- 2 egg yolks
- 6 oz Mascarpone
- 1.75 oz sugar
- 2.75 oz dark chocolate
- 1 tablespoon butter
- Half a glass of Marsala
- 2 tablespoons cream
- Dark chocolate chips
- 2 Meringues

METHOD

1. Take a bowl and a small pot, start melting the chocolate in a double boiler and add the butter.
2. Take the cream and heat it in the microwave (or in a small pot), add it to the chocolate and butter and stir until a homogeneous mixture is formed.
3. Cover the chocolate cream with plastic wrap and let it rest.
4. In the meantime, take the egg yolks and beat them with a whisk until the mixture is light and frothy.
5. Take the Mascarpone cheese and add it slowly, stirring, to the egg yolks, then add the half glass of Marsala.
6. Take 3 bowls. In the first bowl, add 2/3 of the Mascarpone cream.
7. In the second bowl, mix 1/3 of the Mascarpone cream with the entire chocolate cream (you will get chocolate Mascarpone cream).
8. In the third bowl, we compose our last layer! Crumble the meringues on the bottom, add some chocolate-Mascarpone cream and then some white Mascarpone cream. Then add a few chocolate pieces, then the crumbled meringue mixture and we start over again!

Sweet Rice and Lemon Pancakes

Difficulty level: easy
Preparation: 11 min
Cooking time: 5 min
Servings: 2 people
Note: 30 min rest

INGREDIENTS

- 5.5 oz Carnaroli Rice (cooked)
- 1.5 oz Raisins
- Zest of 1 lemon
- 1 pinch Cinnamon powder
- 2 tablespoons Wheat flour
- 1 small Egg
- 1 tablespoon Sugar
- Peanut oil
- Sugar

METHOD

1. Take a bowl and add 5.3 ounces of cooked rice, egg, flour, grated lemon zest, a pinch of cinnamon and a few raisins.
2. Stir the ingredients well until a compact and soft mixture is formed, cover with plastic wrap and let it rest in the refrigerator for 30 minutes.
3. Take a frying pan, add some peanut oil and heat it well but on a low flame. Take the mixture, form small balls with a spoon and fry them on both sides until golden brown. Once the pancakes are golden brown, drain them and roll them in powdered sugar.
4. Serve the pancakes hot!

Chocolate and Avocado Mousse

Difficulty level: very easy
Preparation: 11 min
Cooking time: 2 min
Servings: 2 Stück
Note: 15 minutes rest time in the refrigerator

INGREDIENTS

- 2 tablespoons of sugar
- 5 ounces of avocado
- 1.75 ounces of dark chocolate
- Almond flakes
- Chopped pistachios, hazelnuts or almonds.

METHOD

1. Take the avocado, remove the skin and pit and put the flesh in a blender. Add sugar and blend until the mixture is smooth and without lumps.
2. Set the microwave to 900 watts, put a bowl of chocolate in it and melt it for about 2 minutes, stirring every 30 seconds so it doesn't burn!
3. Combine the avocado cream with the melted chocolate and stir well. Fill the mixture into a piping bag and put it in the refrigerator for about 15 minutes.
4. Take two cup glasses and fill them with the mixture. Garnish with chopped pistachios, almonds or hazelnuts and serve your chocolate and avocado mousse!

Strawberry Milkshake

Difficulty level: very easy
Preparation: 6 min
Servings: 2 people

INGREDIENTS

- 4.5 oz strawberries
- 3.25 oz whole milk
- 0.2 tablespoons sugar
- 2 tablespoons ice

METHOD

1. Take the strawberries, remove the green part and wash them. Cut them into 4 pieces and set them aside.
2. Take the blender, add the ice, then add the milk and the remaining strawberries. Finally, add the sugar.
3. Turn on the blender and blend until the mixture is smooth and creamy.
4. Pour the mixture into a glass and garnish it with the previously cut strawberries.
5. Serve the milkshake cold!

Caramelized Bananas

Difficulty level: very easy
Preparation: 6 min
Cooking time: 11 min
Servings: 2 people

INGREDIENTS

- Water
- 2 oz of sugar
- 7 oz of bananas
- 1.5 teaspoon of butter

METHOD

1. Peel the bananas and slice them into half-inch slices. Set aside.
2. Take a small pot, put in the powdered sugar and melt it over low heat until it turns amber.
3. Add the butter and melt it in the caramelized sugar.
4. Pour in a little water and stir with a spoon to let it evaporate.
5. When the mixture is smooth, add the sliced bananas and let them caramelize for one minute.
6. Enjoy the caramelized bananas hot!

Lactose-free Cocoa and Cinnamon Pudding

Difficulty level: easy
Preparation: 11 min
Cooking time: 4 min
Servings: 2 Stück
Note: chilling time (about 3 hours)

INGREDIENTS

- 9 oz lactose-free milk
- 1 tablespoon lactose-free bitter cocoa powder
- 2 tablespoons cornstarch
- 2.5 oz sugar
- A pinch of cinnamon powder

METHOD

1. Take a bowl and add the sugar, then take a sieve and add the cornstarch and cocoa powder. Add a pinch of cinnamon and sift everything to mix well.
2. Take a saucepan and pour in the room temperature milk. Gradually add the powders that you previously mixed with a sieve. Stir the mixture well to make it smooth and lump-free.
3. Now turn the heat to medium to high and continue stirring until you see the first bubbles. Cook for another 4 minutes and then turn off the stove.
4. Take the pudding molds and moisten them with water. Pour in the hot mixture and let it cool at room temperature for 16 minutes.
5. Now cover the molds with plastic wrap and place in the refrigerator for 3 hours (until the mixture has thickened).
6. Now serve sprinkled with cinnamon!

Pistachio Ice Cream without an Ice Cream Maker

Difficulty level: very easy
Preparation: 16 min
Servings: 2 people
Note: Freezing time (overnight)

INGREDIENTS

- 1 cup (8 fl oz) whole milk
- 1/2 cup (2 oz) shelled pistachios
- 1/4 cup (2 fl oz) water
- 1/4 cup (1.75 oz) sugar
- 1 cup (8 fl oz) heavy cream

METHOD

1. Take a small saucepan and add sugar and water. Light the fire on a low flame. When the syrup boils, turn off the heat and let it cool.
2. In the meantime, take a pitcher and pour the cream and milk in.
3. Pour the syrup into the pitcher with the milk and mix it with a stick blender.
4. Take an ice cube mold (the one you use to make cubes) and pour the mixture into the pitcher. Now take the mold and place it in the freezer overnight.
5. The next day, take the cubes and puree them until they are creamy. Add pistachios and continue mixing.
6. Take an aluminum container, pour the mixture into it and place it in the freezer for 7 hours.
7. Take the ice cream out of the freezer at least 10 minutes before serving to get it creamy!

Raspberry Panna Cotta

Difficulty level: easy
Preparation: 11 min
Cooking time: 6 min
Servings: 3 people
Note: Refrigeration time 4 hours

INGREDIENTS

- 1 cup heavy cream
- 1 tablespoon raspberries
- 0.5 tablespoon gelatin leaves
- 3 ounces powdered sugar
- 1 vanilla bean

METHOD

1. Take a small saucepan and pour the heavy cream, powdered sugar, and the vanilla bean (halved lengthwise) and heat it on low flame.
2. Stir the mixture with a whisk and check with a thermometer that it reaches 80/90 degrees, it should not boil.
3. Meanwhile, soak the gelatin leaves in a bowl with cold water for 10 minutes and then squeeze them well.
4. Once the cream has reached temperature, remove the saucepan from the heat and turn it off. Take a strainer and strain the cream to remove the vanilla bean, then pour the cream into the bowl with the squeezed gelatin.
5. Stir the mixture well so that the gelatin dissolves and then heat it again on the stove for a few minutes.
6. Take 3 molds and put 2-3 raspberries on the bottom, then pour the mixture over it. Let it stand in the refrigerator for 4 hours.
7. To release the panna cotta from the molds, dip the mold for 3 seconds in hot water.
8. Decorate it to your liking!